Masturbation

Masturbation

What Should You Know to Know How To Help

Dr. Richard Thomas

ISBN : 1-4196-3989-7

To order additional copies, please contact us.
BookSurge, LLC
www.booksurge.com
1-866-308-6235
orders@booksurge.com

Masturbation

Table of Contents

Preface

Mt. Carmel Ministries

Dear Reader:

The book you hold in your hand is on a controversial, and, at times, a secret and unaddressed topic in the local church.

The spark for this attempt at addressing this topic from a biblical perspective came from one of my students taking our biblical counseling training program. She gave me an article written by a 22 year youth minister veteran. In that article, he misquoted three Scripture passages in which he concluded that someone could masturbate to the glory of God.

I was enraged that this type of careless biblical exegesis was in print. Thus, I began a journey of personal information and knowledge, combined in a volume that included my counseling experience on the topic. What you hold in your hand is a labor of love for the truth and relevant and practical ways to help counsel men and women involved with this sexual sin.

The manuscript was reviewed by Steve Gallaghar (Founder and President of Pure Life Ministries, Dry Ridge, KY), a valiant warrior battling the problems of sexual sins in the lives of men and women. I owe him a debt of gratitude for his valuable insights and editorial comments. Not all of his suggestions were implemented, but a sufficient amount to make this work more understandable and readable.

I hope the biblical insight will help you understand what

the Bible says, and you will employ the counseling suggestions and guidelines as you work with men, women, fathers, sons, and daughters struggling with this issue.

In the Wonderful Counselor's Name, I am

Rick

Dr. Richard K. Thomas

Fellow with the National Association of Nouthetic Counselors

Member of the International Association of Biblical Counselors

Dedicated to:

A man of God whose
Tireless efforts are evident
In his compassionate labors
To help men and women
Who are shackled in sexual sins
Find freedom in Christ -
Steve Gallagher

Chapter One

Introduction

Perhaps you're a bit nervous, asking yourself what in the world were you thinking when you purchased this book? Or, why did you allow your friend to encourage you to get this book? This is pretty deep stuff, and stuff you just don't sit around and discuss with your best buds! It's not like talking about a close-out sale at your favorite department store or if your favorite sports team will win the pennant!

The "M" topic is uncomfortable for a number of reasons. First, some statistics report over 90% of males do the "M" thing...and the rest who claim they don't are not telling the truth! Second, the "M" thing is not just about guys. Gals are involved. Third, it may be uncomfortable because you are a statistic. You have tried repeatedly to slay this dragon. There has been success, but it only lasts a couple of weeks or months. Then "bam" "M" has its talons in you again and you are defeated. Fourth, perhaps you know of a relative, close friend, son or daughter struggling with the "M" thing. You're concerned and hurt, and they are feeling frustrated and hopeless.

You might be wondering who in their right mind would invest so much time and energy in writing a book about masturbation – there I wrote it! Let me tell you a number of reasons why I wrote this book.

First, except for a few solid but brief articles, I do not know of a serious work in this area. Yet, it is an area that reaps a devastating harvest in the lives of those enslaved to its power.

Second, I want to arouse the Church to confront the back pew where masturbation sits gloating over its converts who stand and sing God's praises. Third, one of the students who is in training to become a biblical counselor showed me an article entitled, <u>Is Masturbation a Sin?</u> I was horrified and angered that a 22-year veteran youth pastor's "opinions" would be given space in a prestigious youth worker's magazine. Fourth, as a certified biblical counselor, my fellow counselors and I unearth the secret practices of masturbation in the lives of men and women, single and married. We see the devastation it creates in the young lives of men and women who were first exposed to pornography at an early age (9-13 years old).

We deal with the fruits of masturbation during marriage counseling. It is not uncommon for masturbation to contribute to marital conflict. Our hearts break when we are working with two people in love who desire to marry, yet one is or has been enslaved to masturbation. Some think that if they can only get married, they will no longer struggle with masturbation.

Marriage does not guarantee freedom from masturbation. Masturbation often continues well into marriage.

With few exceptions, my research reveals the warning of writers to face this issue with courage and compassion. However, the courage and compassion they speak of must "not create an environment of discomfort for those involved with masturbation." Yet, if the priority is to avoid "creating an environment of discomfort," it would seem that courage and environment limits compassion. Perhaps it is not about the environment, but the proper use of the tools of courage and compassion. Instruction is the most effective tool to properly use courage and compassion. Instruction gives courage and compassion the backbone to be bold and understanding in such a way to help those captured by masturbation to exchange their lives of slavery for lives of moral freedom and purity.

My prayer is that this book will,

1. Arouse the reader to understand fully the biblical implications of condoning or ignoring masturbation (Pr. 14:9; 28:13)

2. To identify deviant teachings by those institutions or individuals that teach our young people (1 John 4:1)

3. To bring up our young men and women in the nurture of the Lord (Deut. 6:4; Eph. 6:4)

4. To instruct them to present themselves as living sacrifices which is their spiritual act of worship (Rom. 12:1)

Chapter Two

Prevalent Viewpoints

This chapter is designed to teach you the various positions others advocate about masturbation with the intention of equipping you with an awareness of what these positions believe and teach. The results can increase your effectiveness in working with young people who are flirting with the thrill of masturbation or to help the person involved with masturbation to take every thought captive to the obedience of Christ.

Medical

The Harvard Medical School textbook claims that masturbation is part of the third stage of male development and that masturbation is normal.[1] The writer states, "There is no risk of either pregnancy or disease with masturbation."[2] Masturbation is viewed as a matter of release from sexual tension. The textbook denounces the myths associated with masturbation. "You may have heard that masturbation causes blindness or gives you hairy palms, but this is nonsense. It is a common, harmless activity that gives pleasure, reduces tension, and may be a helpful way for you to delay having sex until you feel mature enough to handle the responsibility."[3]

In the Mayo Clinic textbook, editor-in-chief David Larson affirms the normalcy of masturbation. "There is nothing wrong with masturbation during your teenage years and beyond."[4] It is acceptable because one is allowed to savor the sexual fantasies.

Provided masturbation is not a public display, it should be viewed as normal, acceptable, and not harmful. The book claims that masturbation produces a sensual pleasure and there should be no fear associated with masturbation. Larson states that young people are made to feel guilty because of old unfounded myths.[5]

In *Mosby's Medical, Nursing and Allied Health Dictionary*, Kenneth N. Anderson states that masturbation is normal and harmless.[6] *Hopkins' Medical Information* says, "Masturbation is the safest form of sex possible because it doesn't involve the transmission of bodily fluids from one person to another and carries with it no risk of pregnancy or infection. It is not naughty, evil, or sick. Dr. Klag continues by saying that most researchers assert that masturbation can be a healthy release from sexual tension."[7]

Psychological Community

In the *Psychiatric Dictionary,* copywrite 1996, you can read, "masturbation is usually accompanied by phantasies *(f)* that are of a recognizably sexual nature typically resulting in orgasm. Psychic masturbation (psychology) is also recognized where phantasy alone is sufficient to cause orgasm without direct physical manipulation. The masturbatory act, then, has two aspects – form (physical manipulations) and content (nature of the accompanying or provoking phantasy)."[8]

The conclusion? "Masturbation can be considered psychologically normal during childhood, and is a major avenue for the discharge of instinctual tension. Under present cultural conditions, masturbation is considered psychologically normal during adolescence, and in adulthood when gratification of a physical and emotional relationship with another person is not possible."[9] He cites a survey conducted in the late 1980's where 92% of males and 58% of females masturbated. A more recent survey states 100% of males and 85% of females masturbate.

This author implies that males who suppress the urges of masturbation are maladjusted. "Those adolescents who do not masturbate during puberty show regularly in analysis an especially deep repression of infantile masturbation, threats about which have overwhelmed them with guilt and fear; such patients, incidentally, have a poor prognosis in psychotherapy."[10]

Kaplan and Sadock, who co-authored *Synopsis of Psychiatry*, trace masturbation all the way back to infancy and childhood. The act of self-exploration by the child of his body is normal. This manipulation will lead to masturbation. Because it is viewed as normal at this stage of development, it is viewed as normal at any stage of life. They cite internal conflict in a young person's life for the guilt over masturbation. This conflict consists of the need for sexual exploration and the values and morals instilled either through the society, through the church or through the family unit. The natural way to handle the conflict is masturbation.[11]

Would the psychiatric community make concessions that masturbation can pose a problem? "Masturbation is a psychopathological symptom only when it becomes compulsive. It would be diagnosed as an emotional disturbance, not because it is sexual, but compulsive."[12] Stated differently, masturbation is never the problem, but the obsession or over indulgence of the activity. Kaplan and Sadock go on to state that the compulsion is not the person's fault because when it reaches this level, it is against the person's will. They are a victim of something they cannot control!

In some psychiatric literature, a young person who abstains from masturbation is the one with a problem. "Scruples about masturbation involve some oversensitive pious young people in the danger of suicide. It is anxiety felt about it, not the practice itself that is harmful. Constructive advice on the subject should aim not at stopping the habit – always a futile endeavor – but at removing the attendant anxiety explaining its normality, and diverting anxiety to constructive activities."[13] Craighead and Nemeroft write, "While in earlier historical periods, masturbation was considered a sign of depravity and sinfulness, it is more generally accepted today as a common practice among adolescents and adults, both male and female."[14] A parent reading this material may conclude that their youngster is abnormal because he/she doesn't masturbate, and that, in fact, the parent's scruples and faith-beliefs may be compounding hidden psychological problems!

Religious Community

In the past, religious groups have condemned masturbation as an 'unnatural act" (Rom. 1:27ff). Because masturbation is a solitary action, it brings religious condemnation because God created sexual intimacy between a man and a woman to promote oneness emotionally and physically. From what we have already read in the medical and psychological communities, we should not be surprised that in the religious community the opposition to masturbation has softened.

It very well could be that in the years to come masturbation will be ignored by the church.

Liberal

Because there are no passages in the Bible that discuss the topic of masturbation, and Jesus did not give His opinion on masturbation, He apparently did not consider masturbation of great importance.

When liberals are challenged on masturbation and fantasies, they would typically respond that their moral code is not solely based on the Bible. They integrate the findings of science and medicine. They believe that most sexuality and mental health professionals have concluded that such fantasies are normal and healthy; they are not harmful. Because God created us with sexual and natural attraction, and they are automatic and unavoidable, the individual has no control over these fantasies, and therefore they cannot be sinful. Most liberal Christians would conclude that masturbation is a harmless activity, one that is not particularly sinful. It generates considerable pleasure, and teaches the individual about the body's responses.[15]

Conservative

Although there are no Bible passages directly condemning masturbation, the practice is condemned by conservative

Christian groups. Generally, there are six main approaches within conservative Christianity. These positions are:

[1] One group labels masturbation as a form of adultery. Life Bible Class teaches that masturbation is a violation of one of the Ten Commandments (You shall not commit adultery). They cite 1 Corinthians 7:4 indicating that sexual satisfaction is mutual, not exclusive. Sexual satisfaction outside of the bounds of marriage is adultery and therefore a sin.[16]

[2] Masturbation is a sin because of sexual fantasies. It is not the same as adultery, but it is sinful when accompanied by sexual fantasies and impure thoughts. It is also sin when it becomes habit forming.[17]

[3] Masturbation is a form of impurity and uncleanness. Therefore, it is a sin. Radio Bible Class believes that habitual self-pleasing is contained within the catchall terms lasciviousness, impurity and uncleanness (Lev. 15:16-17; Mk. 7:20-22; 2 Cor. 12:21; Gal. 5:19; Eph. 5:3-5; Col. 3:5)[18]

[4] Masturbation is addictive and a misuse of sexuality. Christ Unlimited Ministries concludes that God created sexuality in order to be enjoyed only between two heterosexual, married spouses. Masturbation is singular and therefore a misuse and sinful. Masturbation is addictive because the individual craves increasingly extreme acts to maintain the same degree of excitement.[19]

[5] Masturbation is against natural law. This argument states that the sexual organs are only for procreation and the mutual satisfaction of both spouses. Any other use is sinful and selfish.

[6] Masturbation is a violation of God's purpose for sex. Dawson McAllister condemns masturbation because

   1. God created sex to overcome man's loneliness. Sex was meant for two people. Masturbation goes against God's purpose for sexuality.

   2. Sexual fantasies almost always accompany masturbation.

3.   Masturbation can damage a person sexually; their future sex life in marriage could suffer.

4.   Masturbation is an unhealthy way to deal with loneliness.

5.   Masturbation is almost always a symptom of a deeper need.[20]

Roman Catholic

In a 1975 declaration given by Pope Paul VI, *Persona Humana – Declaration on Certain Questions Concerning Sexual Ethics*, he states:

"...masturbation constitutes a grave moral disorder..."

"...masturbation is an intrinsically and seriously disordered act...the deliberate use of the sexual faculty outside normal conjugal relations essentially contradicts the finality of the faculty. For it, lacks the sexual relationships called for by the moral order, namely the relationship that realizes 'the full sense of mutual self-giving and human procreation in the context of true love.' All deliberate exercise of sexuality must be reserved to this regular relationship."

"Even if it cannot be proved that Scripture condemns this sin by name, the tradition of the Church has rightly understood it to be condemned in the New Testament when the latter speaks of 'impurity,' 'unchasteness' and other vices contrary to chastity and continence."

"The frequency of the phenomenon in question is certainly to be linked with man's innate weakness following original sin; but it is also to be linked with the loss of a sense of God, with the corruption of morals engendered by the commercialization of vice, with the unrestrained licentiousness of so many public entertainments and publications, as well as with the neglect of modesty, which is the guardian of chastity."[21]

So what can we conclude? What can we learn from these other prevalent viewpoints on masturbation? First, it is easy to set up a straw man and then burn him. We will learn later on just because the word masturbation is not specifically used, nor is it even called a sin explicitly in the Bible, does not mean a student of the Word with proper hermeneutic principles can not implicitly prove masturbation is sinful. Rather than appealing to deductive rationalization, we will appeal to inductive illumination.

Second, many of the arguments within the conservative Christian circles sound biblical, but they lack Scriptural support and contextual argument.

Third, many of the arguments in the liberal and neo-Christian communities follow the medical and psychological research and conclusions. There has been no critical thinking and analysis.

Fourth, the medical and psychological communities have eliminated God in theory and practice.

Therefore,
when you rule out God, you eliminate
a viable, more understandable reason
for the problem and liberating solutions.

Chapter Three

Natural Apologetics

The next two chapters will attempt to provide an apologetic response to the medical, psychological, and religious communities' philosophies that endorse and condone masturbation.

Apologetics involves the mind which attempts to show reason why something is true or false.[1] It is an activity that defends against criticism and distortion by providing evidence for credibility.

Natural apologetics is a means of applying logical conclusions to premises held by others. It involves careful reflection of what someone states as facts and the reasonableness of those statements. Thus far, the previous research can be summarized by the following statements that condone masturbation. They are

1. Masturbation is acceptable because it relieves tension (sexual).
2. There are no harmful effects on the body.
3. There are no harmful effects upon others.
4. Masturbation is better than immoral alternatives.
5. If the majority of the people are involved, it cannot be wrong.
6. There is no difference in enjoying masturbation and enjoying a chocolate bar.
7. Masturbation is natural because it is part of the human development patterns.

8.   Surveys validate masturbation as an acceptable, harmless practice.

9.   Some have no control over the urges and impulses of masturbation. That is the way they are made.

Masturbation is acceptable because it relieves tension (sexual).

The basis for this deduction is that the majority of medical and psychological journals cite this as an acceptable reason for masturbation. But is there support for such a conclusion?

One "dot-com" survey showed the frequency of masturbation of those between the ages 11-35. Those surveyed masturbated an average of eleven times per week. After age 35, the frequency decreased to five times per week.

The word "relieve" means to ease, lighten or reduce. Relieve implies the reduction of misery and discomfort in order to make something bearable. People reading the endorsement by these communities deceive themselves into thinking that masturbation brings relief. This deception is similar to the substance abuser who says that he only needs one drink. One drink may produce the euphoria desired, but the intensity of the euphoria increases and one drink no longer meets the craving. Another drink is added. Could this be a reason for the increased frequency of masturbation by those who participate?

Consider the diagram below.

The circles represent the "bubble-thinking" of justification a person goes through prior to masturbating. The space between the circles represents the time lapse between masturbation. The diagram depicts a reduction of time between events of masturbation. The larger circles indicate the growing appetite of the craving to masturbate and what stimulations are necessary to "satisfy" the activity. The overlapping circles represent multiple times within a given day and the increased stimulation to gain "relief."

Based on this diagram, the fallacy of gaining relief from masturbation is a modification of "the law of diminishing returns" that apply to an addiction. Masturbation doesn't relieve sexual tension, but promotes sexual intensification.

There are no harmful effects on the body.

Most of those writing about masturbation poke fun at the early attempts to prove that masturbation was harmful to the person. Early writers cited baldness, blindness, and hairy palms. As early as 1758, a Swiss physician named Tissot published a treatise claiming that masturbation was the principle cause of mental illness.[2] In 1834, Dr. Syvester Graham wrote that the loss of semen during sex was injurious to health and that masturbation was especially pernicious. To reduce sexual cravings, Graham advised mild foods. The graham cracker was invented. Dr. John Harvey Kellogg created cornflakes to curtail children's inclination toward masturbation. From our vantage point, we see the human folly of such thought processes.

We can tentatively agree that to this point of the discussion there is no scientific proof that masturbation is harmful. But that raises the question of the nature of man. Is man to be considered only material and sexual?

Evolutionists promote the survival of the fittest and the evolving chain of higher development. From a one cell being, man is the pinnacle of the evolutionary chain. Therefore, man is more than a mere body, but a rational and volitional creature. Man can reason, decide, and feel.

Although there are no proven harmful side effects from masturbation on the body, what about the mind and emotions? "Physiologically there seems to be no harm in masturbation, though most psychology text book writers admit that associated guilt and shame afflict millions, especially during adolescence."[3]

Guilt and shame are often explained away by strict and legalistic religious upbringing. However, this would account for a small percentage of fanatics. What can be proposed for the majority who experience guilt and shame from masturbating? The answer is conscience, that innate presence that determines what is morally right and wrong (Rom. 2:15). Though there are no physiological effects, the medical, psychological, and religious communities explain away the effects on the person's mind and emotions. Their explanations are biased and unfounded.

There are no harmful effects upon others.

We read that masturbation is the safest form of sex. There is no transmission of body fluids to cause disease. Because it is a solitary activity, masturbation is harmless to others. Medical and psychological literature upholds the legitimacy of savoring the sexual fantasies through masturbation. When someone cannot find sexual fulfillment with another, masturbation is a viable, harmless alternative.

Because man is the sum total of mind, emotions, and will, is it really possible to fantasize about another while masturbating and there be no harmful effects toward that person? Doesn't what you think have a direct link on how you behave? What if you fantasize about this person, and continue to experience rejection? Do you think that the rejection will compound the thinking and intensify the actions of the forbidden and unattainable? Fantasy is a desire to have something I crave and more than likely cannot have or if I could attain may be disappointed because fantasies are always incredibly more than reality. This is known as lust. Lust is quenchless; its appetite is never satisfied. It always demands more (Js. 4:1-3).

When we lust, we thirst desperately for something that looks like what we want. We don't realize, however, that it is precisely the opposite of what we really need. In fact, it can kill us. Masturbation hurts other people because the person who masturbates withdraws, isolating himself. He lies and deceives to avoid discovery. He is fearful, and what was once a close relationship and open communication are now drastically affected. Masturbation hurts other people.

Masturbation is better than immoral alternatives.

Many believe that "it is better to masturbation(e) than live with excessive obsession with sex....and it is better to masturbation(e) than risk falling into more serious sexual immorality involving another person."[4] The other serious sexual forms of immorality would be adultery, fornication, bestiality, rape, incest, or homosexuality.

The problem with this line of reasoning rests on the concept of quantifying. Those who argue this way are attempting to quantify one action as less significant, therefore acceptable, in contrast to others deemed unacceptable. By what standard would one conclude the degrees of wrongness? Would that standard be universally agreeable?

For example, there is a difference in fines between a speeding ticket and a meter violation. There is even a difference in fines among speeding ticket violations based on the number of miles-per-hour over the limit. Everyone would agree and this would be nearly universally recognized. However, there is still a level of wrongness for both the speeder and parker, and for the two speeders. One cannot argue leniency based on circumstances. Therefore, the lesser of two wrongs, is still wrong!

The color gray is white colored with a drop of black.
So it is with masturbation.
Masturbation is the drop of black to moral purity.

If the majority of the people masturbate, it cannot be wrong.

What is it that makes the majority seem right? The belief that the majority is right stems from subjective surveys of human opinions, unscientific statistical information and summations, and generalizations by the medical and psychological communities.

James Dobson falls into this trap. He writes, "Between 95 and 98 percent of all boys engage in this practice (masturbation) – and the rest have been known to lie. It is as close to being a universal behavior as is likely to occur."[5] His conclusion? "My advice is to say nothing after puberty has occurred. You will only cause embarrassment and discomfort."[6]

The flaw with this logic is likened to the nursery school game of "Follow the Leader." It stems from a blind, accepting belief in the statements and conclusions of men esteemed without scrutiny (Mt. 15:14). It is trust in 'experts' without critical assessment. People may be sincerely passionate and believable...and sincerely wrong (Ps. 118:9, 146:3).

There is no difference in enjoying the pleasures of masturbation and enjoying the pleasures of eating a chocolate bar.

Someone argues, "When someone eats his favorite food, he is enjoying the pleasure of the feel and the taste of the food. Is it sinful to enjoy eating a chocolate bar? No. It only becomes a sin if the activity and the pleasure of eating become something which crowds out God, becoming an end to itself rather than being seen as a blessing from a loving God. When a person masturbates, his body will respond to the pleasurable physical stimulation that it's being given. ...the act becomes an experience of blessing from the Lord."

How do you handle this type of reasoning? The problem is the right of pleasure. This argument presents the pleasures of masturbation as some God-given right! The pleasure is acceptable as long as we don't cross "a line" – a line that is defined by the participant in a subjective mental and emotional state. This understanding of pleasure feeds the flesh and results in self-gratification.

If pleasure is the determining factor in life, why would

anyone go to work? Live within a budget? Obey the speed limits? Work on conflict or repair relationships?

Our society and its morés demand obedience to a code. You get a traffic ticket when you speed because you disobeyed a posted speed limit sign. Your car is repossessed because you violated the contractual agreement for payment. You lose your job because you fail to show up for work. Some citizens may be relativistic at heart, but they live in a structured society. The issue is not pleasure, but obedience. Obedience feeds the spirit that results in glorifying God, not self.

Masturbation is natural because it is part of the human development patterns.

This argument comes from Freud's model of human sexuality. Because a baby will tend to explore his body, discovering his fingers and toes, it is logical to explore his sexuality in a similar way. If a baby does this, he will experience an instinctual sexual pleasure. This is part of his human growth and development. Other writers indicate that it is normal for such practices to continue into adolescence and adulthood.

If this logic is true, that a baby who explores his body and discovers the pleasures of instinctual sexual pleasure, and it continues through adolescence into adulthood, one could argue that breastfeeding should continue to age 12...or 26....or 42? Why not continue self-discovery of the world around me, as babies do, by putting things in my mouth?

Your response is one of credulous sneering! "No grown person would do that!" "And why not?" I might ask. "Because," you would reply, "they have grown up and have acquired knowledge about such things." "Precisely." I would comment, "and the same reasoning holds for other areas of development; can it not be equally applied to masturbation rather than suggesting it's normal to continue throughout adulthood and even encouraging it?" Why does this pattern linger on while the majority of other developmental patterns do not?

Surveys validate masturbation as an acceptable, harmless practice.

Much of the encouragement to masturbate is derived from surveys. These surveys indicate the frequency of masturbation per week by gender and age groups as well as the percentage of males and females participating. We live in a society where numbers project acceptability or feasibility. We return to the majority syndrome.

First, these surveys are not scientific. Second, the "data" gathered is subjective – it is the opinion or experience of an individual. Third, the conclusion drawn by the populous endorsing a certain practice as harmless is seriously flawed. For example, legalizing marijuana would be well received by the majority. It wouldn't hurt anyone; it is harmless. We know that reasoning is unsound. Drug rehabilitation counselors and law enforcement agencies know that legalizing marijuana would lead to the use of other hard drugs and influence violent crimes.

Surveys are not reliable. They are only indicators. Remember the headlines of an election long ago, "Dewey Wins." History records Truman holding up the headline with a big smile!

Some have no control over the urges and impulses of masturbation. That is the way they are made.

We are told in literature that masturbation is something that people do who cannot have a normal relationship with another. We read that those who become extreme are not responsible; they have no control over their impulses or urges. They do not have a sexual problem, but a psychopathological problem. Their thinking is obsessed with stimulants that result in masturbation. But they cannot control this!

In Steve Gallagher's book, *At the Altar of Sexual Idolatry*, he writes that sexual sins are hidden. The person involved with sexual sins (masturbation) takes great efforts to hide this participation because of fear of discovery, hurting others, losing a job, wife or children. It is not like someone addicted to substance abuse. Sooner or later the problem manifests itself through broken health, job loss, violence, or financial ruin. But sexual sins are controllable by the participant. How do we know this? The person involved may be a bank president, television preacher, senator, grandparent, son or daughter and you might never know or suspect.[7]

**It is not a matter of being out of control,
but choosing to be out of control.**

It's a matter of a person abandoning passions to defective reasoning. In almost every other area of life, this person can control passions when driving a car and another cuts him off, or speaking to an unbearably cruel employer, or a host of other situations...abandoning passions to defective reasoning.

Chapter Four

Biblical Apologetics

When Jesus was challenged by the Pharisees in John 8, Christ followed the Jewish principle of calling two or three witnesses to validate His statements. In chapter three, a number of witnesses from natural apologetics were summoned to testify. From a logical point of view, they bring to bear significant weight for consideration to counter claims that masturbation is innocent and harmless.

In this chapter, we will call an additional ten witnesses from the Bible. The following statements demand an apologetics. These statements are drawn from the religious community. They are

1. The word 'masturbation' is never mentioned in the Bible. Therefore, it is not a sin.
2. There are a number of Scriptural 'boundaries' that promote masturbation as a means to glorify God.
3. Guilt and shame are the by-products of an oversensitive religious community.
4. Morality is not restricted to definition or practice by the Bible alone.
5. God made us as sensual beings. Masturbation brings pleasure. God's intention of enjoying our sensuality finds its fulfillment in masturbation.
6. Masturbation is permissible when a person cannot have a physical relationship with another.
7. We can trust the conclusions of the science and medical communities.

8. Masturbation is a private, solitary activity, and does not involve other sins.

9. Masturbation is natural because God made us as sexual beings and has given us permission to explore our sensuality.

10. As long as the mind does not focus on lustful fantasies, masturbation is acceptable and harmless.

The word 'masturbation' is never mentioned in the Bible. Therefore, it is not a sin.

Michael Ross of Focus on the Family was asked if masturbation was a sin. His response was: "To be honest, the Bible seems to be silent on this issue."[1] He continues, "...it appears less significant to God than most of us."[2]

Another cites, "There are no passages in the Bible that discuss this topic directly. Jesus did not give His opinion on masturbation. Although He gave hundreds of instructions to help us govern our lives, He apparently did not consider the topic of human sexuality of great importance."

Can this really be the case? Who created Adam and Eve, male and female? Who gave command to Adam and Eve, before the Fall and after the Fall, and to Noah, after the flood, to be fruitful and multiple? Who recorded precisely, graphically, and pointedly the sexual sins and punishments of Sodom and Gomorrah? Who wrote about the beauty of love, marriage, and sex in the Song of Solomon? Who wrote about the husband and wife love relationship in Ephesians and Colossians? If God was not interested in human sexuality, He seems to take a lot of time, space, and words on the topic!

The argument is because the word "masturbation" is not used in the Scriptures, one can conclude that it is not a sin. Would those who hold such a position also hold that one day Christ will return for His chosen ones with a shout, the voice of an archangel and the trumpet of God as insignifant (1 Thess. 4:13-18)? Entire theological systems have been developed around a concept represented by a word not found in the Bible – the

Rapture! We are commanded in 1 John 3:3 to purify ourselves because of His imminent return (rapture).

One can critically explore the Bible and find no direct prohibitions against smoking, drinking or drugs – in fact, no direct statements naming them as sin! But through proper interpretation, one can conclude from Scriptures that these items harm the body God has created and defiles the Temple of the Holy Spirit who lives therein.

For the conservative, we believe in a monotheistic God who operates in three roles: Father, Son, and Spirit. The word Trinity is not found in the Bible, but the absence of the word does not mean the concept is invalid. There are numerous examples of the Trinity such as the creation of the world, the baptism of Jesus, the crucifixion of Christ, and YOUR salvation.[3]

One cannot argue that because the word "masturbation" is not found in the Bible, and that Christ never addressed that issue, the Bible permits its practice.

There are a number of Scriptural 'boundaries' that promote masturbation as a means to glorify God.

Dale Kaufman writes, "What are the boundaries which the Word of God sets forth for something like masturbation? In what contexts is the act acceptable, and when does it 'cross the line' into a sinful activity?"[4] He cites three passages of Scriptures he calls boundaries that permit, and even parade masturbation as a means of glorifying God.[5]

How would you respond to this? Scripture is provided? How can it be wrong? The problem with this line of reasoning is misguided hermeneutics and bending interpretation rules to support a conclusion. Remember 2 Peter 1:20-21:

But know this first of all, that no prophecy of Scripture is a matter of one's own interpretation, for no prophecy was ever made by an act of human will, but men moved by the Holy Spirit spoke from God.

There are two fundamental concepts which must be followed to reach the proper interpretation. First, someone studying the Bible must understand that God's revelation is progressive in nature. God did not reveal His entire program.

Through increments, God unveiled what man needed to know or what man was able to comprehend and obey. "The Bible did not fall from Heaven all in one piece. From Moses to John, its composition took about sixteen centuries, during which time the divine truth was manifested with increasing clarity. The appearance of the sun makes an excellent illustration of this truth: dawn approaches progressively; then the sun bursts forth on the horizon, gradually but steadily mounting to its zenith, while its light steals nearer and nearer to illumine the whole landscape."[6]

A second fundamental concept which must be followed to reach the proper interpretation is a latter revelation cannot contradict a previous revelation. Stated differently, there is complete unity in the Scriptures. Subsequent revelation usually amplifies or clarifies earlier revelation, but never opposes. When Scriptures are made to say something that was not intended, usually poor or lazy hermeneutics are applied.

Kaufman wants us to believe that masturbation is permissible because of the citation of three Bible passages (1 Cor. 6:19-20; Phil. 4:8; Col.3:17). The New Testament often amplifies on previous Old Testament revelation. What earlier revelation hinted that masturbation was acceptable?

What is a solid procedure that guarantees the right interpretation and understanding of the passage in harmony with the totality of the Bible?

Consider the diagram below:

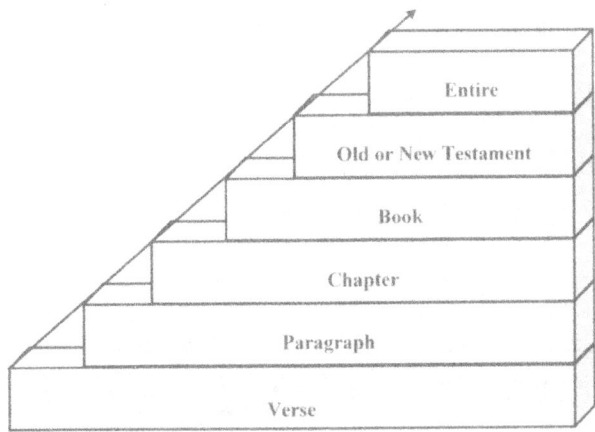

You must examine the verse within the paragraph. The paragraph dwells within a chapter. The chapter lives within the book that reflects the author's intention, purpose, and design. The book resides within a Testament (Old or New). The Testament must live harmoniously with the entire revelation (Bible).

Guilt and shame are the by-product of an oversensitive religious community.

"Scruples about masturbation involve some over-sensitive, pious young people in the danger of suicide."[7] James Dobson, noted Christian psychologist responds by saying, "...so, what should parents say to their kids about this subject? My advice is to say nothing after puberty has occurred. You will only cause embarrassment and discomfort."[8]

From an article entitled, "Masturbation and the Bible", the writer records how psychology responds to guilt: "Physiologically there seems to be no harm in masturbating, though most psychology text book writers admit that associated guilt and shame afflict millions, especially during adolescence. This guilt is usually blamed on strict and legalistic religious upbringing and Victorian prudishness about sex."⁹

Are guilt and shame really by-products of an over-sensitive religious community? Can guilt and shame be reduced to mere manipulation? Or are we failing to see the purposes of and the distinctions between guilt and shame?

A biblical definition of guilt is a legal or judicial term that implies criminal responsibility in the eyes of a court of law, whether human or divine. There are three Greek word groupings that provide helpful insight on the concept of guilt. First, *aitia* means the grounds, cause, reason, charge or motive for the guilt (Mt. 19:3, 27:37). Second, *eleychoo* means to bring to light, expose, set forth, convict, convince and provide evidence for *aitia* (1 Tim. 5:20, 2 Tim. 4:2, Titus 2:15). Third, *enochos* means liability, deserving of a penalty in keeping with the charge and evidence (Mt. 5:21; Js. 2:10).

Guilt, therefore, is

exposing someone's actions,

identifying the reason (s), and

assessing an appropriate punishment

to restore the offender to God and his fellow man.

Guilt is a direct result of sinful actions (Job 10:14; Ps. 32:5). The Holy Spirit convicts of sin and the human mind interacts with this convicting work to produce guilt. People can be used by God to produce guilt in the lives of others using the Word of God with the sole purpose of restoration (Gal. 6:1).

On the other hand, shame is the feeling someone

experiences because of another who has mistreated him and the conflict remains unresolved. There is one Greek word for shame (aischune) which means disgrace or dishonor. In classical Greek writings, shame carried the idea of ugly or disfigured. In the Old Testament, the word is most prominently used in conjunction with God's judgments upon His enemies. Biblical characters who dealt with shame were Joseph, Daniel, and our Lord.

So what are we to conclude? Guilt is not the by-product of an over-sensitive religious community. It is not solely attributed to strict or legalist religious upbringing and Victorian prudishness. It is a God-given barometer that accurately describes and diagnoses one's spiritual, mental, and emotional well-being.

Morality is not restricted to definition or practice by the Bible alone.

"Liberal Christians typically do not base their moral code solely on the Bible. They integrate findings of science, medicine, etc., including research into human sexuality. Most sexuality and mental health professionals have concluded that masturbation is normal and healthy."[10]

This argument reflects the problem of source. All truth is not God's truth. Bill Goode, former Executive Director of the National Association of Nouthetic Counselors, now present with the Lord, expounds on the misnomer of all truth is God's truth. "Rather than saying, 'All truth is God's truth and bringing all kinds of suppositions and theories into the church, it is time we looked at the sources that some are calling truth."[11]

What are the sources of truth people rely upon? There is empirical truth or discoveries from human studies. This would include knowledge gained by laboratory and other testing. This may prove helpful, but what is proven and is called "truth" or "fact" today may be proven wrong tomorrow. Although empirical data may be of great benefit, we can never be sure about it or equate it with revelation.

"One medical doctor said he was told in his last year that 'fifty percent of what is taught to you as fact today will be proven wrong in six to ten years, and no one knows which 50 percent that is. A more recent graduate of medical school spoke up and said, 'Today the time interval for changing those things we once called 'fact' is from one to three years.[12]

Another source of knowledge is theories and opinions produced by reason. Reason is a gift of God, but reason is affected by sin. Apart from the Bible, no one can have absolute certainty that he or she is reasoning correctly. Whatever the source of knowledge coming from reason, it has limitations. The natural mind cannot bridge the span between natural and supernatural. Reason works with the data available. Even if one has accurate data, the natural mind is suspect in reaching the right conclusions. Why? "The deceitful nature mind seeking to study the deceitful nature mind, personality, and habits is bound to come short."[13]

So morality must be bound by definition and practice to the Bible alone. The Word of God is the only infallible rule for faith and practice. It is inspired (2 Tim. 3:16). It is all sufficient to teach, reprove, correct, and train.

God made us as sensual beings. Masturbation brings pleasure. God's intention of enjoying our sensuality finds its fulfillment in masturbation.

We addressed a form of this reasoning in Chapter Three with natural apologetics. I would like to consider a second line of reasoning. The premise is God designed us to enjoy pleasure. In our previous argument, we proposed God calls us to obedience. We are enjoined by Paul to, "Be imitators of me, just as I also am of Christ."[14] The Christian is called to obedience, and he is called to imitating Christ.

What would this look like, instead of a life of pleasure? To imitate Jesus, we must walk like He walked (1 John 2:6). Jesus denied the flesh and its pleasures. When tempted with hunger, he refused to enjoy the pleasures of turning stones into bread (Mt. 4:3-4). He told the disciples that the pleasures of home and family were foreign to Him (Jn. 8:20, Mk. 3:35). He denied the pleasures of Heaven and took on the form and fashion of a man

(Phil. 2:5ff). He absorbed the pain and suffering of crucifixion and did not flee from the will of God (Heb. 12:1-2).

Our culture and its influence have proclaimed the search for and enjoyment of pleasure and avoidance of long-term gratification. Yet the chief end of man is to worship God, enjoy Him forever and to glorify Him...not self.

Masturbation is permissible when a person cannot have a physical relationship with another.

Dr. Robert Campbell writes, "Masturbation can be considered psychologically normal during childhood, and is a major avenue for discharge of instinctual tension. Under present cultural conditions, masturbation is considered psychologically normal during adolescence, and in adulthood when gratification of a physical relationship and emotional relationship with another person is not possible."[15]

There are several ways to respond biblically to this argument. First, the saint's conduct is not determined by what culture determines as acceptable. This philosophy was clearly displayed, along with its horrific consequences, in the days of the judges (17:6, 21:25). Second, it seems as if the relationship is reduced to the most primitive foundation, namely the physical. The privilege of physical intimacy is reserved for marriage and marriage alone! (1 Cor. 7:1; Heb. 13:4). Our culture overemphasizes physical attraction and experimentation with sex to determine compatibility. These premises are diametrically opposed to the biblical worldview.

Finally, and most important, the heart of this argument is degraded lust. The permission to masturbate if one cannot have a physical and emotional relationship with a person demonstrates that within this person's heart is an idol of lust and self. A person trapped by such reasoning would retort, "But I really love her, but she doesn't love me." The type of love that condones masturbation as a substitute for God's marital design and personal purity is animalistic. It is lustful. The desire is for personal gratification. The focus is self. The object is "my needs, wants, and desires," and because culture, science, and psychology ordain it as permissible, the practice hides behind godless justification.

Craig Rowe developed a chart that shows how someone with an idol thinks, how this thought process affects the person's life, and how to dethrone the idol. The chart's concept is presented in abbreviated form here. Keep the chart before you as you read the following explanation.

False Beliefs	Resulting	Work, Friends, Time, Priorities Money Emotions	Genuine Belief	Resulting
If I...	...Then	♡ Pleasures Lusts Passions Desires Cravings	The Bible says...	I must...

Because I cannot have a physical or emotional relationship with another, masturbation is permissible. (thought process and subsequent practice). This person is driven by lusts, craving, desires, passion, and pleasure of the act. This reasoning affects

1. friends (he fantasies about female friends or co-workers)
2. money (he may purchase adult entertainment for greater stimulation)
3. emotions (he will experience guilt, shame or anger)
4. time (other things could have been accomplished).

This person needs to be taught what the Bible says and given counsel on how to practice the new belief system.

We can trust the conclusions of the science and medical communities.

This argument has appeared, in one form or another, twice before - once under natural logic and previously in argument number four. We have addressed it by affirming the fact that there is only one source of truth, that the premise of "all truth is God's truth" is inaccurate and untrustworthy.

Let's dismantle this premise from another point of view. Regarding our topic at hand, scientific testing consists of surveys, public opinion, and cultural acceptance establishing norms. But common sense reminds us that with each new generation, what the previous generation used to determine acceptance is subject to change with a high degree of probability. The results concluded in any generation using these standards are empirical which accounts for the varying outcome.

Consequently, hope placed in the "experts"[16] disappoints, and is biblically prohibited. Psalm 118:9 and 146:3 state, it is better to take refuge in the Lord than to trust in princes. Do not trust in princes, in mortal man, in whom there is no salvation. Why?--Because the "experts" devise their truth using human intellect. God is eliminated. That is why Proverbs 3:5-6 cautions against such practice when it says that we are to, *"trust in the Lord with all your heart, and do not lean on your own understanding. In all your ways acknowledge Him, and He will direct your paths straight."*

Masturbation is a private, solitary activity, and does not involve other sins.

It is hard to imagine that you can throw a rock at a glass house and it won't break. That is what this premise is saying. Because a man or woman masturbates in the quiet darkness of their bedroom or bathroom, this action is permissible because it doesn't involve any other sin. Masturbation is a glass house!

Is it possible to masturbate and not commit any other sins? James 4 reminds us that:

For whoever keeps the whole law and yet stumbles in one point, he has become guilty of all. For He who said, "Do not commit adultery," also said, "Do not commit murder." Now if you do not commit adultery, but do commit murder, you have become a transgressor of the law.[17]

Consider the following concept.

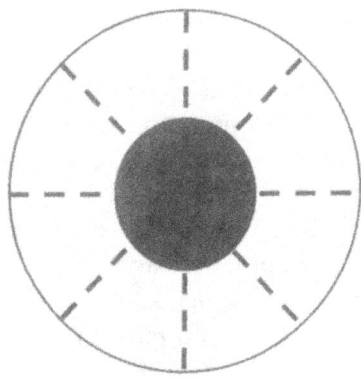

    Below is a circle within a circle. The smaller circle (color black) represents the sin. The outer circle is divided into smaller pie shape compartments. Each compartment represents sins associated with the inner circle.

    The smaller circle will represent the act of masturbation. Is it a solitary sin, isolated from the rest of life, and relationships with God and man?

1.   There would be the sin of an uncontrolled thought life (2 Cor. 10:4-5)
2.   There would be the sin of lust (James 1:14-15)
3.   There would be the sin of making provisions for the flesh (Rom. 13:14)

4. There would be the sin of deception (Gal. 6:7-8)
5. There would be the sin of an undisciplined life (Titus 2:11-12)
6. There would be the sin of stewardship of time, body and resources (1 Cor. 6:19, Eph. 5:15-16)
7. There would be the sin of dishonoring of parents (Ex. 20:12)
8. There would be the sin of selfishness (Rom. 15:2-3)
9. There would be the sin of coveting (Ex. 20:17)
10. There would be the sin of idolatry (Ex. 20:3-4)[18]

One must conclude, therefore, that although masturbation is committed in the privacy of and control of one's own environment, as are other sexual sins, the privacy issue must not be construed as permissible. Masturbation, like most all other sins, is a sin that leads to other sins.

Masturbation is natural because God made us as sexual beings and has given us permission to explore our sensuality.

"Some of the leading Christian psychologists in the nation have said that masturbation is a normal function that, unless carried on into marriage, usually proves to be harmless. It may be normal for fallen man to masturbate but that does not make it acceptable in the eyes of a holy God. These natural passions are called the lust of the flesh. God does not, nor will He ever, condone the carnal and selfish gratification of masturbation. He created sexuality as a way for two married people to express love for one another and to enjoy mutual satisfaction. Sex outside of this context becomes something sordid and dirty."[19]

There are several points of biblical apologetics to consider. First, it is true that God created male and female as sensual and sexual beings. The obvious reason is given in Genesis 1:18-25 where Adam needs a companion. The uniqueness and distinctions are for pointed reasons, especially if this couple is to obey the Lord and be fruitful and multiply. Second, one cannot argue from the silence of Scriptures, science, medical, philosophy or psychology that exploration of one's sexuality and subsequent masturbation is God's design. Third, if we are going to credit God with creation, then we have to blame God for the results of self-exploration and all that comes from such activity. Question: Where would one take a young person to prove either explicitedly or implicitedly that when God put the hormones in the body, He granted permission, and even endorsement, for self-exploration and masturbation?

As long as the mind does not focus on lustful fantasies, masturbation is acceptable and harmless.

Is it possible to masturbate and not have lustful fantasies? I guess anything is possible, but I do not believe it is probable. **If one was truly focusing on God**, as described in the Westminister Confession of Faith,

There is but one only living and true God, who is infinite in being and perfection, a most pure spirit, invisible, without body, parts or passions, immutable, immense, eternal, incomprehensive, almighty, most wise, most holy, most free, most absolute, working all things according to the counsel of His own immutable and most righteous will, for His own glory; most loving, gracious, merciful, long-suffering, abundant in goodness and truth, forgiving iniquity, transgression, and sin; the rewarder of them that diligently seek Him; and withal most just and terrible in His judgments, hating all sin, and who will by no means clear the guilt. God hath all life, glory, goodness, blessedness, in and of Himself; and is alone in and unto Himself all sufficient, not standing in need of any creatures which He had made, nor deriving any glory from them, but only manifesting His own glory in, by, unto and upon them; He is the alone fountain of all being, of whom, through whom, and to whom, are all things; and hath sovereign dominion over them, to do by them, for them and upon them, whosoever Himself pleaseth. In His sight all things are open and manifest; His knowledge is infinite, infallible, and independent upon the creature, so as nothing is to Him contingent or uncertain. He is most holy in all His counsels, in all His works, and in all His commands. To Him is due from angels and men, and every other creature, whatsoever worship, service or obedience He is pleased to require of them.[20]

If one was truly focusing on the Lord Jesus Christ, *The One who is Creator of all things, the preserver of all things, came to Earth to His own, manifested God to mankind, manifested man to God, He pardons sins, raised from the dead, destroyed the works of the Devil, rewards His saints, the saint's High Priest, and soon coming King.*

If one was truly focusing on the Holy Spirit, *who is the Spirit of the Living God, Spirit of Him who raised Jesus from the dead, the eternal Spirit, the Spirit of glory, the Spirit of life, the Spirit of wisdom, the Spirit of wisdom and understanding, the Spirit of counsel and power, the Spirit of Truth, and the Comforter; who is eternal, omniscient, omnipotent; who strives against sin, inspired the Scriptures, convicts of sin, righteousness and judgment to come, restrains sin, regenerates, illumines, anoints, baptizes, seals, fills, intercedes and sanctifies.*

It is highly improbable that one focused on the Trinity would be able to move the body to sexual stimulation that leads to masturbation. Rather, someone truly focused on the Trinity will echo the words of the Bible saints:

Then I said, "Woe is me, for I am ruined! Because I am a man of unclean lips, And I live among a people of unclean lips; For my eyes have seen the King, the LORD of hosts."[21]

So I gave my attention to the Lord God to seek Him by prayer and supplications, with fasting, sackcloth and ashes. I prayed to the LORD my God and confessed and said, "Alas, O Lord, the great and awesome God, who keeps His covenant and lovingkindness for those who love Him and keep His commandments, we have sinned, committed iniquity, acted wickedly and rebelled, even turning aside from Your commandments and ordinances.

"Moreover, we have not listened to Your servants the prophets, who spoke in Your name to our kings, our princes, our fathers and all the people of the land.

"Righteousness belongs to You, O Lord, but to us open shame, as it is this day—to the men of Judah, the inhabitants of Jerusalem and all Israel, those who are nearby and those who are far away in all the countries to which You have driven them, because of their unfaithful deeds which they have committed against You.

"Open shame belongs to us, O Lord, to our kings, our princes and our fathers, because we have sinned against You. "To the Lord our God belong compassion and forgiveness, for we have rebelled against Him; nor have we obeyed the voice of the LORD our God, to walk in His teachings which He set before us through His servants the prophets.

"Indeed all Israel has transgressed Your law and turned aside, not obeying Your voice; so the curse has been poured out on us, along with the oath which is written in the law of Moses the servant of God, for we have sinned against Him.[22]

But when Simon Peter saw that, he fell down at Jesus' feet, saying, "Go away from me Lord, for I am a sinful man, O Lord!"[23]

...and a host of other Bible characters, who, when they focused on God, did not seek sensual pleasure, but discovered whom they really were, men filled with sinful attitudes and practices. Their response led to godly repentance and sorrow.

Steve Gallagher writes, "Masturbation revolves around lust and fantasy, neither of which God approves. Furthermore, it is masturbation that opens the door to further bondage. To attempt to justify it spiritually is just more self-deception."[24]

Chapter Five

What Does The Bible Say?

"Closing Arguments" – a term that describes the final summary remarks made by the prosecuting and defense attorneys. The prosecuting lawyer will review all the evidence presented by his office and remind the jury of their responsibility to render a guilty verdict.

The defense attorney creates doubt in the jury's mind by disputing the evidence and passionately proclaims that the prosecution has not met the burden of proof. The defense lawyer may interject, "if there is reasonable doubt, you must find the defendant 'Not Guilty'."

Applying this analogy to masturbation, the prosecutors (science, medicine, philosophy, religion, and psychology) have not met the burden of proof that masturbation is permissible, harmless, normal, and the safest form of sex. The jury is ***not*** out on this issue. I trust that by the end of this chapter, the verdict will be rendered concisely and effectively that there is reasonable doubt to consider masturbation as acceptable, and there is ample evidence to label masturbation as sinful.

Exhibit A – Biblical Language

Biblical scholars often conclude that masturbation is sinful because of biblical language. Scholars indicate that masturbation falls under the categories of lasciviousness, impurity, uncleanness, or fornication. Is this assertion true?

After researching these terms, the following summary

is offered. *Lasciviousness* is mentioned in passing without further definitive elaboration. *Immorality* includes a wide range of implications, but seems to lean towards anything in general that was immoral. *Impurity*, similar to immorality, offers little understanding for the inclusion of masturbation. *Unclean* presents the strongest biblical language that justifiably concludes masturbation as a sin.

The word 'unclean' is a compound word in the Greek language. It is comprised by the letter 'a', and the word *katharos*. *Katharos* means to cleanse, cauterize, and open a wound to remove the germs and bacteria. The letter 'a' negates the meaning of the root; *akatharos* means not to cleanse, to allow the germs and bacteria to remain in the wound. *Katharos* belongs to a family of words which reflects cleanliness in regards to physical, cultic, and ethical purity.

Leviticus uses the word unclean a number of times. It is used by the priests proclaiming a leper clean or unclean. From the *International Dictionary of New Testament Theology*, Colin Brown writes, "...sexual processes are regarded as making a person unclean (emission of semen {15:16}), menstruation (15:19), unhealthy discharge (15:2, 25), intercourse (1 Sam. 21:5ff), adultery (18:20), rape (Gen. 34:5), homosexuality (18:22) or other sexual aberrations (18:6ff). The emission of semen is repeated in Lev. 22:4 and Deuteronomy 23:10-11.[1] Let's consider these verses.

Leviticus 15:16-17 (NASB)

[16]*Now if a man has a seminal emission, he shall bathe all his body in water and be unclean until evening. [17]As for any garment or any leather on which there is seminal emission, it shall be washed with water and be unclean until evening.*

Several observations must be made. First, how seminal emission is not stated. It may be nocturnal in nature, or it may be attributed to stimulation. Second, the law demanded that he bathe the body in water, symbolic of defilement, along with any articles stained by the emission. Third, there is a timeframe for this defilement – until evening. Fourth, there is no prescribed offering to be made. Although there is no specific sacrifice, there are steps of restoration to community life. Therefore, one must conclude that seminal emission violates the law and there is a prescribed way to be restored. God spoke clearly of His displeasure of it.

Leviticus 22:4-7 (NASB)

⁴*'No man of the descendants of Aaron, who is a leper or who has a discharge, may eat of the holy gifts until he is clean. And if one touches anything made unclean by a corpse or if a man has a seminal emission ⁵or if a man touches any teeming things by which he is made unclean, or any man by whom he is made unclean, whatever his uncleanness; ⁶a person who touches any such shall be unclean until evening, and shall not eat of the holy gifts unless he has bathed his body in water. ⁷But when the sun sets, he will be clean, and afterward he shall eat of the holy gifts, for it is his food.*

Again, several observations must be made. First, the priesthood, along with the laity, is included in the instruction. Second, specific restrictions are made regarding the evening sacrifice and participation. The offender was not permitted to partake of the "holy gifts" unless certain conditions were met. Third, as stated before, he had to bathe his body with water. Fourth, the time restriction was until sunset. Provided he had bathed and met the other requirements, he would be permitted to participation after sunset in the holy offerings.

What additional insight is discovered? If the person cannot eat the holy gifts, then that person is unacceptable to God. Because of the seminal emission, he cannot approach God until the prescribed time and through the prescribed means. Therefore, seminal emission is sinful.

Deuteronomy 23:10-11 (NASB)

¹⁰*"If there is among you any man who is unclean because of a nocturnal emission, then he must go outside the camp; he may not reenter the camp. ¹¹But it shall be when evening approaches, he shall bathe himself with water, and at sundown he may reenter the camp.*

Again, observation of the text is important. First, this text specifically says 'nocturnal emission'. The other texts are not that specific. "Wait," you say, "the other texts must be referring to nocturnal emissions, right?" Can we really conclude that?

Leviticus 15:16-17 appears to be discussing more active sexual participation, as well as Leviticus 22:4-7. Besides, the context is different in this passage as Moses speaks to the second generation and is providing an abbreviation of the Law.

Second, the same prohibition is given as in the Leviticus passages. Third, the same procedure for restoration to the community is cited.

The biblical language is strong enough to conclude, by inductive and deductive study, that masturbation is included under the word unclean.

Another Greek word is often referred to as inclusive of masturbation. Citing from an article entitled, "Masturbation and the Bible," the author states "...fornication (*porneia*) is a broad word in the New Testament actually encompassing all forms of sexual immorality."[2]

Exhibit B – Biblical Feelings

We have read numerous times in the text how authors advocate that people who experience guilt over masturbation do so because of rigid, religious, old-fashioned, and Puritan dogma. Guilt is not the result of doing something wrong; it is the by-product of values and beliefs imposed by another.

As I sit here and write about guilt, I am reminded of how words have taken on new meaning, or how our culture has redefined terms. I often here my sons quip, "That's a bad ride." Bad is redefined as good. Or, "That is so lame," meaning weak. Or, "That was wicked," meaning excellent or awesome. Our culture, through psychology and philosophy, is redefining guilt to mean something bad, unhealthy, inhibiting – something that is imposed upon one by others (external). Was guilt always viewed this way?

The Bible has much to say about guilt. Let's do a brief word study and biblical survey on guilt, and by so doing, recapture the essence of the purpose and the reason for guilt – the feeling experienced by millions who masturbate.

By definition, guilt is a legal or judicial term that implies criminal responsibility in the eyes of a court of law, whether human or divine.

How do people respond to guilt? From Genesis 3:7-13, we can conclude four unbiblical ways to respond to guilt. First, Adam and Eve covered up their guilt. Second, Adam and Eve attempted to hide from their guilt. Third, Adam and Even tried to avoid their guilt. Finally, Adam and Eve blamed each other.

The "experts" are telling us that guilt is imposed upon another. This burden is unhealthy and causes greater anxiety and problems. Biblical counselors understand that others can produce guilt through manipulative tactics in order to control the person. How big of a slice is this compared to the entire guilt pie? Consider the other sources of guilt.

People can be used by God to produce guilt in the lives of others using the Word of God with the sole purpose of restoration (Gal. 6:1). Biblically, and ultimately, it is the Holy Spirit who convicts of sin and the human mind interacts with this convicting work to produce guilt. Guilt is a direct result of sinful actions (Job 10:14; Psalm 32:5). People often bear the unnecessary guilt because of lack of faith (Hosea 10:2). People can live guilt free (Job 33:9). But how?

Guilt must be acknowledged before God grants forgiveness (Hosea 5:15). Forgiveness is available for all sin and associated guilt (1 John 1:9; Psalm 32:5). God has graciously provided the appropriate sacrifice for guilt. In the Old Testament, it was the guilt offering (Leviticus 5-6). In the New Testament, it is Jesus Christ (Isa. 53:10).

Guilt, therefore, and as a rule, is not something external, but a God-given internal mechanism used by the Holy Spirit, in conjunction with the human mind, to bring to light an attitude or action displeasing to the Creator and Redeemer. Consequently, when an unnatural act or violation of God's design[3] occurs, my conscience measures that act to an awareness of truth and understanding.[4]

**Guilt feelings are generated
when the action fails to meet the standard of truth.**

If someone believes the lie that masturbation is harmless and acceptable, guilt is numbed and dulled.[5] Guilt is controlled by further lies and deeper sinful sexual practices. Guilt will always be there, like the deafening roar of a lion caged in a sound proof and padded room. You look through the glass, you see the guilt, but you no longer can hear it. You think you have tamed it.

Again, guilt is God's way of alerting a person something is wrong - whether a believer or an unbeliever. Guilt is God's loving, warning system to check to see if you are in the faith!

Exhibit C – Biblical Focus

We carefully laid out how it is impossible, and therefore improbable, that someone can masturbate thinking about and praising God for sensations they are experiencing through masturbation. We agree that during the early days of adolescence and puberty a young person's hormones are inflamed. We agree that undesirable data from sex education classes is disseminated. We further agree that far too many parents avoid the topic, hoping that somehow, someway their child's sexual understanding and feelings will fall into place with the least amount of fallout.

I remembered a Walt Disney film called, *Getting Even with Dad*. Danzin played a con looking for one more big score. McGally played the estranged adolescent who was dropped off, unannounced and in the middle of his father staging a heist, for a week with his dad.

In one scene, Danzin took his young son to an art museum. Danzin had his son stand very close to a huge portrait. Asking his son what he saw, he heard, "A bunch of dots." Closing his son's eyes, he moved the child back a significant distance, and upon the boy opening his eyes, gasped at the beauty he had been to close to see.

Similarly, those involved with masturbation are too close to honestly see they have an idol in their hearts. Their focus is too blurry and distorted. These spiritual cataracts often blind the persons before necessary surgery is performed because they received their eye examinations from the community of the blind!

The focus of masturbation is self. Masturbation makes provision for the flesh to gratify the flesh. It longs to experience the pleasures of sin for a moment. The experts tell us that masturbation is a solitary experience. They are absolutely correct because masturbation is all about "ME". It is selfish.

Permit me to describe selfishness and ask this question, "Does this portray someone who masturbates?"

Someone who is selfish replaces biblical love. He is only concerned about their needs and drives. A selfish person is more concerned about what he needs, wants, desires from God or others rather than what they can give to God and others. Selfishness is reluctant to receive and act upon God's will. Selfishness superimposes one's own will over God's will. Selfishness does not see certain practices as sinful. It minimizes certain practices. Selfishness does not set its heart on things above. Selfishness often cannot recognize biblical love for its true essence. It is confused and disoriented. Selfishness does not take into consider the effects of its decisions upon others.

Now, does this portray someone involved with masturbation? Self-love is never commanded or encouraged. Self-love is not biblical love. Can we safely conclude that masturbation is selfishness, therefore, sinful?

Exhibit D – Biblical Patterns

John White, in his book, *Eros Defiled*, presents the concept of design as a reason to understand masturbation as sinful.

In Eros Defiled, I wrote about masturbation with compassion. I still have compassion for the victims of masturbation, but the time has now come for me to challenge the views that prevail and to call Christians to face reality. Masturbation is sin. It is not grave sin, not nearly as serious as pride, or cruelty, or even unkindness. But still it is sin.

Let me state my reasons for calling it sin at all. It is sin because sexuality was not given us for that purpose. In masturbating, we use our bodily parts for a purpose God never intended for them. To say that the release of sexual tension justifies it is what my grandmother would have called 'all my eye and Peggy Martin' – or what logicians might call spacious reasoning.

My first argument, then, for calling masturbation sin is what could be called the argument of design. My body is mine only in the sense that I am responsible for its proper use. I am its steward. For what was my body designed? The Westminster Confession asks a similar if not identical question. "What is the chief end of man?" The answer the authors give is, "Man's chief end is to glorify God and to enjoy Him forever."

Paul expresses the same end for our bodies. He concludes, "So glorify God in your body" (1 Cor. 6:20). The argument I have been using from chapter three onward concerns the offering of our bodies to God as an act of worship. In the NIV version of Romans 6, Paul even mentions the parts of our bodies, saying, "Do not offer the parts of your body to sin, as instruments of wickedness...offer the parts of your body to him (God) as instruments of righteousness. For sin shall not be your master" (Rom. 6:13-14).

My body was not designed to masturbate. My body was designed to be used exclusively to glorify God. To use it in any other way is to rob God of something that is His by right, for there are no morally neutral actions.[5]

We have offered four compelling pieces of evidence for you to deliberate upon. If there is the slightest element of doubt that masturbation is permissible, harmless, normal, and the safest form of sex, you must render a verdict that masturbation is sin before the eyes of a holy Creator and Redemptive God.

Chapter Six

Helping the Single

A young woman was brutally attacked as she returned to her apartment late one night. She screamed and shrieked as she fought for her life, yelling until she was hoarse -- for thirty minutes -- as she was beaten and abused. Thirty-eight people watched the half-hour episode in rapt fascination from their windows. Not one so much as walked over to the telephone and called the police. She died that night as thirty-eight witnesses stared in silence.

Another's experience was similar. Riding on a subway, a seventeen-year-old youth was quietly minding his own business when he was stabbed repeatedly in the stomach by attackers. Eleven riders watched the stabbing, but none came to assist the young man. Even after the thugs had fled and the train had pulled out of the station and he lay there in a pool of his own blood, not one of the eleven came to his side.

Less dramatic, but equally shocking, was the ordeal of a woman in New York City. While shopping on Fifth Avenue in busy Manhattan, this woman tripped and broke her leg. Dazed, anguished, and in shock, she called out for help. Not for two minutes. Not for twenty minutes. But for forty minutes, as shoppers and business executives, students and merchants walked around her and stepped over her, completely ignoring her cries. After literally hundreds had passed by, a cab driver finally pulled over, hauled her into his taxi, and took her to a local hospital.

In the above true stories, what do you think prevented people from helping? Fear of being assaulted? Not knowing how to help? Believing their efforts would make no difference. Not wanting to get involved? Uncomfortable? Awkward? Inconvenience? Not my problem? Someone more qualified to assist? These responses sound pathetic in retrospect, but are very real when you are in the throes of the trauma!

I believe that when someone brings the sin of masturbation to light and is seeking help, we respond similarly – with superficial, pithy clichés. We advise the person to pray about it, to get involved in a small group or support group. Or we'll give them a book to read and offer to meet with them if they want to call and schedule a time (perhaps praying all the while that they won't call!). We'll see them in church and ask them how they are doing to which they respond fine, because the timing of the question is not conducive to the environment, hindering in-depth honesty. We may even begin to see this person on a regular basis, feel excited and energized, reading favorite Scriptures and "pumping" up their spirits. But week after week, he returns defeated and discouraged. Like a tire with a slow leak, we blow in some more Bible verses and hope next week he will feel better.

You might be saying right now, "Rick, you sure seem pessimistic. What else can a person do in cases like this? It's tough, and it's not the easiest sin to deal with!" And I ask, "What sin is?"

If we don't biblically, practically, and relevantly provide solid answers, they will find other avenues for help. All they have to do is go to www.amazon.com and click on "self-help." They will find 25,906 options (and counting), or www.barnesnoble.com and find 38,041 "self-help" options (and counting). We need to be reminded that God has given us everything pertaining to life (how to be saved) and godliness (how to live saved).

This chapter is devoted to sharing tools, resources, and methodologies the counselors at Mt. Carmel Ministries have found effective in helping those who masturbate. I will present them in the following fashion.

Christ calls us to love the Lord our God with all our hearts, mind, soul, and strength.[1] If the object of our affections, energies, and focus does not love the Lord in this way, then we love something or someone else, which is idolatry. Therefore, masturbation is a matter of self-worship. The person involved in masturbation loves himself with all of his heart, mind, soul, and strength. Research and reflection on this concept shows numerous different resources in each of these areas to restore the object of worship to the Lord God. Stated differently, there are biblical resources that can help the person who masturbates to return his heart, mind, soul, and strength to loving God, rather than himself.

Before suggesting these resources, biblical counselors know they have a built-in starting point. It is called gathering data. This is crucial. If we are going to help this person effectively glorify God in his body, we must ask questions, record answers, ask questions from those answers, record more answers, study the answers, identify the performance problem issues, and look for the pre-conditioning problems. If we fail to execute meticulously this task, the best we can hope for and the best we can offer to this person is behavior modification.

Gathering Data

What kind of data am I looking for? I would encourage you to use a PDI[2] or develop a similar questionnaire. The PDI will provide a wealth of information that will generate further questions and data. Below is a list of questions that have proved helpful.

1. When did the person first become involved in masturbating?
2. What were the circumstances?
3. What was the frequency when he first started?
4. What is the frequency now?
5. What was the stimulus when he first started?
6. Where did he find or get the stimulus?
7. What is the stimulus now?
8. Where does he find or get the stimulus now?

9. Is the stimulus visual (pictures, pornography, etc.), mental (fantasies), or emotional (loneliness, dating and frustrated, pity party)?
10. What media influences are present?
11. Does he watch a lot of prime time television?
12. Does he rent questionable videos?
13. Does he subscribe to cable?
14. Does he have internet access?
15. What is the purpose of internet access?
16. Does he receive pornographic e-mails?
17. Does he have 'blockers' or security devices'?
18. Is he married? Is there regular intimacy with his spouse?
19. Is he single? Is he dating? Is he engaged? Is he sexually active with this person (Whether dating or engaged)?
20. Using the Total Structure Chart[3], probe to see the extent of this sin into other areas of his life.

Addressing the HEART

Person's Motivation

The word <u>motivation</u> comes from the Latin word that means to move. It pictures someone with inner drive, impulse, and intentions. Motivation is the causation for a particular course of action. It is what drives a person to be the best in the classroom, sports, education, vocation, etc.

Motivation is central to all of life. It determines why you do what you do.

Someone wrote a fable about a dog who loved to chase other animals. He bragged about his great running skill and said he could catch anything. Well, it wasn't long until his boastful claims were put to the test by a certain rabbit. With ease, the little creature outran his barking pursuer. The other animals, watching with glee, began to laugh. The dog excused himself, however, by saying, "You forget, I was only running for fun. He was running for his life!" That does make a difference! Motivation is the most important factor in everything we do

When we speak of the heart, we are not referring to the organ that sustains breath and life. The heart is used to represent desire or focus, motivation. In Hebrew literature, the word heart refers to the hub of life, that which is central to life, significant, meaningful.

When working with someone enslaved to masturbation, it is vitally important to clarify why the person wants to deal with this sin. Many involved with masturbation have the wrong reasons for stopping. Wrong motivation places the person on a slippery slope, clawing his way to the top, only to slide back into the pit of sin and despair. What are motivations that people have for wanting to conquer masturbation?

1. I want to stop masturbating so I can be free from sexual sin.
2. I would like to feel better about myself.
3. I desire to have a better marriage.
4. I yearn to be a good example before my children.
5. I need my wife to trust me again.
6. I can't stand the guilt and shame.
7. I am worn-out pretending to be something I am not.
8. I am tired of hiding.

At face value, these seem to be excellent reasons why a person would want to address the masturbation issue. But let me ask you, "If we were able to provide biblical solutions to help achieve the reasons cited above, do you think God has this person's heart?" I would propose to you, "More than likely not." The person has changed his behavior.

What should be the motivation to abandon the sin of masturbation? The motivation is to become a fully committed follower of the Lord Jesus Christ. Paul reminds us in First Corinthians 10:31 that whatever we are involved in should be done to the glory of God. The motivation is to obey Christ and glorify God.

I learned this lesson very pointedly. After working with a man for a number of weeks, he was experiencing great success. He was having victory over sexual sin in his life. Then he fell and with great remorse wept on how he wanted victory over sexual sin. For the next two months, a cycle began to develop of victory and then sin, repentance, remorse and resolve. I despaired in helping him so I consulted Jay Adams' Fifty Failure Factors.[4] I reviewed the numerous motivational factors to bring about change.[5] Then it was as if I was able to hear what this man was saying by the Holy Spirit..."I just want to be free from sexual sin...I just want to be free from sexual six...I just want to be free from sexual sin." That was the problem. The focus was wrong. The heart was improperly motivated. What this man needed was to please God, to glorify God, to obey God. When he changed the focus, things began to turn around.

Another area under the worship of the heart is the concept of holiness or sanctification. I have concluded that many people struggling with life dominating sins, especially sexual ones, have a distorted concept of the holy life. I believe this is attributed to their repeated attempts to resolve the sin issue.

The Cycle

The person becomes weighed down by his sin. Overwhelmed by guilt, he seeks help. He begins to see a glimmer of hope that he can change. He renews his efforts to moral purity. His efforts begin to pay a dividend. He feels good about his progress. But something happens that influences a personal decision to return to masturbation. He feels defeated and resign. He justifies his actions and for a period continues in the sin. Then he becomes weighed down by their sin. Overwhelmed by guilt, he seeks help and the cycle revolves.

Because these people have experienced the "stop n' go" righteousness, they come to believe that they have to live perfectly. They develop a standard of righteousness that is performance based. They measure their relationship to God as good when they remember to do everything they are supposed to do. The slightest short fall shoves them into the valley of despair. "So what's the use," they say. "I might as well enjoy the sensual pleasure of masturbation. I just can't win." They have equated sanctification with perfectionism.

The average Christian believes in progressive sanctification. This means a process. Paul himself spoke of his progressive journey in Philippians 3:8-14 when he wrote,

⁷But whatever things were gain to me, those things I have counted as loss for the sake of Christ. ⁸More than that, I count all things to be loss in view of the surpassing value of knowing Christ Jesus my Lord, for whom I have suffered the loss of all things, and count them but rubbish so that I may gain Christ, ⁹and may be found in Him, not having a righteousness of my own derived from the Law, but that which is through faith in Christ, the righteousness which comes from God on the basis of faith, ¹⁰that I may know Him and the power of His resurrection and the fellowship of His sufferings, being conformed to His death; ¹¹in order that I may attain to the resurrection from the dead. ¹²Not that I have already obtained it or have already become perfect, but I press on so that I may lay hold of that for which also I was laid hold of by Christ Jesus. ¹³Brethren, I do not regard myself as having laid hold of it yet; but one thing I do: forgetting what lies behind and reaching forward to what lies ahead, ¹⁴I press on toward the goal for the prize of the upward call of God in Christ Jesus.

Triumphs over masturbation are momentary temptations with eternal victories. This is the sanctification process. We must impress upon the hearts and minds of those wrestling with masturbation that there is no "perfectionist zone" that if sustained for a time results in eradication of the problem. The sin nature is ever present, the call is to faith, and victory comes from obedience.

Addressing the MIND

Person's Thinking

One of the crucial areas to agree upon with the person besieged with masturbation is calling it sin. You may think that this should not be a difficulty. You fail to realize that advocates from the medical, psychological and Christian community are asserting its normalcy, acceptableness, and harmlessness. So more than likely, someone coming to you will be unsure and uncertain to its sinfulness. Chapters three, four and five provided ample instruction regarding the sinfulness of masturbation.

Another area of the mind will be that of controlling the thought life. Fantasies are often the stimulus of masturbation. Dreaming, wishing, imaginations of a woman's anatomy, fueled by explicit pornographic pictures, trigger the battle in the arena of the mind between purity and uncleanness. Dr. Amy Knicely says, "You do what you do, and you feel what you feel because of what you think." How true.

Is the thought life that powerful? What we think determines behavior.[6] The Bible tells of Isaac who told others that Rachel was his sister. The text clarity reveals the power of his thought life when it records that he was afraid of what the men may do to him on account of her beauty. He thought that they would kill him and take Rachel.[7] The condition of the mind produces corresponding actions (Genesis 26:6-7).

The stimulants for the person enslaved to masturbation are often the thought life. The images "download" into the hard drive of the mind and can be accessed anytime and anywhere... and no one ever knows. The fundamental exercise of any Christian is to prepare and guard his mind. Every Christian can do and must guard his mind. There are a number of things we can do to help.

Teach the person he can control his thought life.[8] Teach the person to invite God to test their thought life.[9] Take time to help him practice warfare thinking.[10] Have the person write out promises of God's power, provision, and presence to utilize during times of temptation. Numerous other teaching topics and homework assignments can be used with each different situation.

Another area of the mind is determining and dethroning the idols of the heart. There is particular thinking that occurs before a person masturbates. This thinking leads to justifying the action.

For example, someone may say that God is forgiving so the person justifies the action. Another may say that there is still time to change. After this act of masturbation, I will really try hard to change. Still another may say that it is just this once giving credence to the act. Or someone may say they need relief from the stress and pressures mounting inside them.

Look for numerous "reasoning" idols that foster the sin of masturbation. Take each one and show how the action affects other areas of his life. Now, search the Scriptures diligently to find the biblical replacement thought that leads to righteous behavior.

Another area to consider is the person's relationship to the Holy Spirit. This means that you are convinced the person is a believer. Consider using the following progression in developing the person's relation to the Holy Spirit unto maturity.

1. Teach the person what it means to be *controlled by the Spirit* – Eph. 5:18
2. Teach the person what it means to be *taught by the Holy Spirit* – 1 Cor. 2:13
3. Teach the person what it means to be *led by the Holy Spirit* – Romans 8:14
4. Teach the person what it means to be *sanctified by the Holy Spirit* – 2 Thess. 2:13
5. Teach the person how to *walk in the Spirit* – Gal. 5:16
6. Teach the person what it means *to bear the fruits of the Holy* Spirit – Gal. 5:22-23
7. Teach the person what it looks like *to live by the Holy* Spirit – Gal. 5:25

Addressing the SOUL

Person's Design

The Latin language defines design as "to mark out" plus "sign". Perhaps this is where we derived the concept of designer clothes where the signature of fabric, colors or even the designer's name is stamped upon the collection.

There are a number of designs for the soul of the person who is involved with masturbation. Some of these designs will be discussed under disciplines. However, there are three designs that seem to be recurring in this area of masturbation.

The first design is to recognize the warning signs of masturbation. James writes:

[13]*Let no one say when he is tempted, "I am being tempted by God"; for God cannot be tempted by evil, and He Himself does not tempt anyone.* [14]*But each one is tempted when he is carried away and enticed by his own lust.* [15]*Then when lust has conceived, it gives birth to sin; and when sin is accomplished, it brings forth death.*[11]

There are six warning signs we must teach to the one

involved with masturbation.[12] First, temptation is close when the person feels God is unfair or unloving. God cannot be blamed for human circumstances, consequences, or conditions. The reason God cannot be blamed is two-fold. One, God is holy. He cannot be solicited to devise evil. He cannot be invited to think evil. Therefore, the person can trust God. God never has a moral lapse. He never lies and He never has inappropriate actions. Second, God cannot be blamed because He is loving. His love is never harmful, never manipulative, and never selfish.

The second warning sign that temptation is near is when the person is drawn away from a God-ordained authority. Temptation attempts to draw out or away from safety. Temptation lures with the promise of something better and deserved. People are drawn away from authority by questions of doubt, an unbeliever's statement, another's testimonial, or peer pressure over personal views.

Temptation paints the picture of masturbation as harmless, pleasurable, designed by God, and a host of other reasons already discussed. I should ask, when tempted, "Would all of my God-given authorities encourage me in this?[13]

The third warning sign that temptation is nearby is when there is a strong desire for self-gratification contrary to the Word of God. As a rule, sexual temptation starts with a look. Eve saw that the tree was pleasant, David saw Bathsheba, and each saint battles with the lust of the eyes. The strong desires come from the world that provides reasoning and justification to participate, the flesh who stirs human emotions seeking pleasure and avoiding pain, and the devil that fuels the mind with deliberate choices to reject truth. When temptation wins, the person is enslaved to its lusts. There will be deception (Eph. 4:22), enslavement (Titus 3:3), mastery (1 Peter 1:14), and dictatorship (2 Tim. 3:6).

The fourth warning sign is to allow the desire to dominate the thought life. Domination takes time. This portrait of time is likened to the conception and birth process. The fifth warning sign is when ways are developed to act out the temptation. The spiritual birth of sin is a serious consideration of an action. The birth of sin is seldom a quick action. The mind determines the course of action. Jezebel considered a course of action that would allow her husband, Ahab, to secure the plot of land belonging to Naboth.

The sixth warning sign of temptation is rejecting and substituting God's divine pattern: happiness for joy, lust for love, tranquility for peace, pleasure for discipline, and selfishness for perseverance.

Besides teaching the warning signs of temptation, show how one can tame temptation. Open your Bible to Matthew 4, and read the Temptation Scene of our Lord Jesus Christ. Observe the fifteen ways someone can tame the temptation to masturbate.

1. Expect temptation when you commit yourself to the work, word, or will of God – 3:15 (Baptism of Jesus)

2. Expect temptation when you are experiencing the favor of God – 3:17 (well-pleased)

3. Expect temptation when you are Spirit-led – 4:1

4. Anticipate new spiritual blessings when you tame temptation – 4:2 (numerology of "40")

5. Know the greatest area of vulnerability – 4:2 (Hunger for Christ)

6. Understand that your position in Christ does not grant you special privileges to sin – 4:3 (if you are the Son of God).

7. Allow God to meet real legitimate needs – 4:3 (turn stones to bread)

8. Live by the principles of the Word of God – 4:4,7,11 (It is written)

9. Know how to use the awesome power of God's Word – 4:4 (live by every word)

10. Guard against embracing cultural beliefs – 4:5 (pinnacle of Temple)

11. Accurately interpret the Scriptures – 4:6 (misquotation of Ps. 91:11-12)

12. Learn contentment by recounting the faithfulness of God – 4:7 (do not test God)

13.   Remember the transitory nature of life – 4:8 (kingdoms of this world)
14.   Pursue eternal, life-changing goals – 4:10 (worship and serve God only)
15.   A single victory moves you to the next level of spiritual challenge – 4:11 (Satan left for more opportune time)

Work through each of the fifteen ways to tame temptation and place that principle in the context of taming masturbation. There are powerful ways to implement each truth.

Another design that must be addressed is that of leisure. We discovered relaxation without purpose increases the temptation to masturbate. We also discovered that the mental justification of "I've worked hard, I deserve to," or "I'm tired and this will help me relax" abounds.

Sounds like relaxation is now work. That's no fun! Someone said that an idle mind is the devil's workshop. Relaxation must have a purpose. If we are to do everything to the glory of God,[14] relaxation is part of everything! Relaxing without a purpose or focus leads to boredom. Let's say I am going to hang with some friends...and we're just going to chill....you know...just hang! I believe the next decision will arise out of boredom. But if I am going to chill with the 'buds' to discuss the theory of existentialism (just kidding), then I have a purpose and focus. Without purpose or focus, I turn inward and selfish.

I encourage singles to ask the following question, "How will this glorify God?" "As a result, how will this help me grow?" "In what specific ways do I see myself encouraging others in their walk with God?" You could probably add more questions. The point is not to be discouraged and cry out, "I'll never be able to relax," but to make appropriate changes where relaxation can become an obstacle to masturbation.

There are other designs of equal importance. I would be re-writing the Bible to comment on them. From our vantage point, the above designs are reoccurring and must be addressed.

Addressing the STRENGTH

Person's Disciplines

Each person you deal with that comes to you for help in

gaining victory over masturbation is an individual and the performance and pre-conditioning data vary.[15] Again, we have found the following basic areas.

First, restore the love of fellowship with God through daily devotions. A daily devotion is investing time with God through a medium He honors and blesses – His Word. Too many saints are using devotional ding-dongs, filled with creamy fluff that contains little to no spiritual nutritional value! I would recommend two resources to restore daily devotions around the Word. [1] *The One-Year Bible*, which contains readings in the Old Testament, New Testament and Psalms-Proverbs. The person can select from the Old Testament, or the New Testament, or the Psalms-Proverbs. Now to prevent mere mindless reading, have the person record what the passage was saying, how he understands it in light of his situation, and what specific ways he can they think of to obey what they read. [2] *The Walk of Repentance* is a workbook that consists of 24-weeks of daily Bible lessons. Each week is thematic in nature. This is a powerful tool to reestablish daily fellowship with God.

Second, evaluate with whom the person associates. It is obvious that the person should cut off associates who are involved with the promotion of or active participation in masturbation.[16] However, I would advocate that evaluation be made for those associates who are having the same struggle. They say misery loves company. The concept of small-sin groups is growing.[17] There will be little accountability, confrontation, and exhortation by its membership towards a fallen comrade. There will be mercy, tenderness, empathy, and sympathy. There will also be a pseudo self-righteousness if one of its members had a good week compared to another's tale of woe. Proverbs tells us that he who walks with wise men will be wise.[18] Is the person I am going to counsel with living in victory? Is the person I am going to counsel with having moral lapses? These are questions of great weight. Answering them may be the difference between sustaining an appetite for sweets and developing an appetite for strong meat!

Third, there will be a need to establish biblical

accountability. Biblical accountability is best achieved one-on-one, not in groups. Groups provide safety in which to hide. Honesty may hide behind shame and embarrassment. And if transparency is shared, should we not be cautious about who hears such honesty?[19]

If you are working in a church environment, look for spiritually qualified men and women to be mentors. If you do not have spiritually qualified men and women, develop them through discipleship and mentoring.[20] Link the person involved with masturbation to an older, godly, same sex person. Provide solid biblical materials to work through on a daily basis. Guide the mentor and person to establish a daily check-in time, and a weekly face-off time to discuss and apply the materials.

At times, our counselors are unable to network with the local church to secure such assistance. As counselors, it is difficult to establish a set time for phone calls. One way we attempt to compensate for this predicament is the use of e-mail. I personally have counselees who e-mail me daily with prescribed materials. It is not the best situation, but until churches understand the significance of their role in helping, we use the resources available to us.

Fourth, for several weeks have the person record his time in increments of 30 minute blocks. The purpose of the time log is to evaluate the use of time.

6:00-6:30 AM	Woke and took shower
6:30-7:00 AM	Breakfast
7:00-7:30 AM	Drove to work

Time is often wasted, or it expands to fill the tasks at hand. If the person thinks he has the rest of the night to do his laundry, what will he do between washing and drying loads? Once you have identified the time loss patterns, continue using the time log and add a task scheduler.

6:00-6:30 AM	Woke and took shower	AM TASKS
6:30-7:00 AM	Breakfast	Drop off mail
7:00-7:30 AM	Drove to work	Drop off dry-cleaning
7:30-8:00 AM		Devotions
8:00-8:30 AM		Employee Project

The task scheduler provides a space to list daily tasks and to assign blocks of time for accomplishing the task. Because there is lack of discipline in the person's life (especially the use of time), this exercise will restore structure and produce great benefits for personal purity. At the heart of this is restoring self-control through discipline.

I hope that these suggestions, based on our limited experience and knowledge, will assist you as you work with those who long for sexual freedom from masturbation.

Chapter Seven

Helping the Married

This chapter will be relatively short for one simple reason. How you work with a married person will be very similar to how you work with the single person (Chapter 6). But there is one distinction, namely the person is married. This raises a fundamental question of why someone who is married masturbates.

This chapter will not elaborate on all the possible reasons, but will focus on two reasons why masturbation may take place in a marital union. They are [1] viewing pornography or [2] there is unresolved conflict between them.

It is not uncommon to discover that one or both marriage partners were involved in pornography prior to marriage. In fact, good pre-marital counseling will unearth the presence of this vile element and deal with it before marriage! Pornography is a mental-emotional stimulus for masturbation. It is the candle of fantasy lit by human lust. Pornography distorts God's design of lovemaking. The marriage bed is defiled in the mind. This distortion often leads to dissatisfaction. The images created by pornography cannot be achieved in marriage because they are not real. Yet the deception that the pictures locked inside the person's mind can be real only deepens the sin and frustrates the one involved with the sin. When the mate cannot measure up to the mental fantasy, the lure of pornography and masturbation is more exciting and thrilling.

The second reason why a spouse masturbates is unresolved

conflict. In marital counseling, often the husband complains of "not enough sex".[1] If prolonged, the husband labels his wife as "frigid."

For my doctorate, I did a paper on the concept of the frigid wife for a Family and Marriage course. After my research, I concluded that unresolved conflict accounted for a large portion of unsatisfying sex relations in marriage. The most intimate act of communication is the most vulnerable. When other lines of communication break down in a marriage (mental, emotional, vocal), the wife will find it difficult to give herself lovingly and freely to her husband in the physical realm. Her actions are one of self-preservation. She doesn't want to feel used. Connections have failed in the primitive areas essential to marital concord. Consider the diagram below. If the couple were given a pyramid, how would they position it?

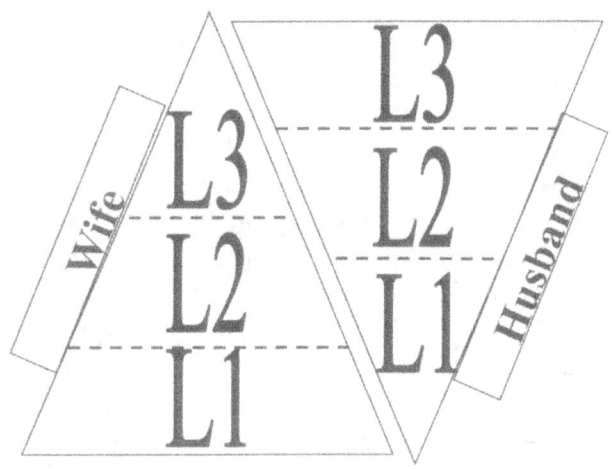

L1 for the wife is spiritual oneness. For the husband, it is sexual union. L2 for the wife is communication of heart, mind, and soul.[2] For the husband, it often is the same. L3 for the wife is physical union. For the husband, it is the spiritual dimension. To summarize, it is typical for the husband to value the sexual union over the spiritual union. It is typical for the wife to value the spiritual union over the physical. When there is unresolved conflict, often a large chasm occurs in the marital relationship and one mate will seek solace through masturbation. Therefore, it is vital for the health of the marriage to perform thorough data gathering, looking for the unresolved conflicts. The lack of physical intimacy (unless there is the presence of pornography) should not be the sole criteria for evaluating the marital union. Lack of intimacy reflects other discord at much deeper levels.

Chapter Eight

Material Resource List

Where does one begin to look for solid biblical resources to help the counselor help the counselee? Of course, we agree the Bible is the final authority, and that the Bible is the sole source of instruction. But, if this is the first time someone comes to you with this counseling need, you may feel a bit overwhelmed. Even if you counsel in this area with some degree of frequency, each person involved with masturbation is an individual; his data is unique to his situation and will require a different approach. I can remember giving one husband some material that was over-powering and incredibly inappropriate for this man. I quickly learned to understand my data and develop a resource materials list.

First, let me provide five organizations you can trust to provide solid counseling resources.

P & R Publishing
PO Box 817
Phillipsburg, NJ 08865
800-631-0094

Pure Life Ministries
PO Box 410
Dry Ridge, KY 41035
888-293-8714

Resources for Changing Lives
1803 East Willow Grove Avenue
Glenside, PA 19038
800-318-2186

Sound Word, Inc.
PO Box 2036
Chesterton, IN 46304
219-548-0933

Timeless Texts
9127 Bertram Ct
Huntersville, NC 28078
800-814-1045
MCM has utilized a variety of resources from these distributors with great satisfaction for timely delivery and scholarly, practical, and relevant materials.

Printed Literature
Books by Steve Gallagher, Pure Life Ministries
Fork in the Road
At the Alter of Sexual idolatry
Walk of Repentance
Breaking Free from the Power of Lust

Books by Jay Adams, Timeless Text
Winning the War Within
Christ and Your Problems
Godliness Through Discipline

Books from Resources for Changing Lives and P & R Publishers
In the Arena of the Mind by V. Vandegriff
Pornography: Slaying the Dragon by David Powlison
The Enemy Within by Kris Lundgaard
Through the Looking Glass by Kris Lundgaard

Cassette Tapes from Sound Word, Inc.
Victory Over Addictions by Dr. Ron Allchin (2-part)
Helping People Overcome Selfishness by Lou Priolo
Stress management by Dr. Bob Smith
Helps in Preventing Moral Failure by Randy Patten
Counseling Those Enslaved to Lust by Dr. John Street
Helping Men Overcome Life Dominating Lust by Dr. John
Street
Maintaining Purity by Dr. Wayne Mack
Overcoming Sexual Lust by Dave Edgington
Pornography: Slaying the Dragon by Dr. David Powlison

Study Guides
Idols of the Heart by Dr. Craig Rowe
Selfishness by Lou Priolo

From Dr. Wayne Mack, Homework Volume I

1. Anger
2. Blame shifting
3. Loneliness
4. Planning and Priorities
5. Pride
6. Self-Control (Discipline)
7. Structuring Your Life for Biblical Change

I trust that you will check out these resources. I am confident they can increase the effectiveness of your ministry to those involved with masturbation.

Chapter Nine

A Final Word

One author writes, *"It's time to stop standing on the sidelines, hoping that somehow our kids will get the right information and act on it in the right way. We must be proactive, getting over our own fears and uncomfortableness, and initiate discussions with our sons and daughters. We must do what is our God-given responsibility as parents and youth leaders; we must help teens navigate the stormy waters of their sexuality. May God help us all to do so, in the right way and in the right time."*

I believe this book is a better way than what is currently being propagated. I believe this book has come at the right time. Never before in our ministry have we experienced so many people involved with masturbation. And I believe that God will help us to do so. We must completely, totally, and thoroughly search the Scriptures. Then we must, allow the Holy Spirit to teach, lead, and guide us. Now we are superiorly equipped to guide those whose passions are enslaved to masturbation to walk by and in and live by the Spirit of the Living and True God.

Sources Quoted

Chapter One

[1]Kaufman, Dale: "Is Masturbation A Sin." Youth Worker Magazine, Nov/Dec issues, 2001.

Chapter Two

[1]Komaroff, Anthony L., M.D., Editor-in-Chief: Harvard Medical School, Simon and Schuster, New York, New York: 1999, page 1026 What is the title of the book being used?

[2]IBID, Komaroff, page 1033

[3]IBID, Komaroff, page 1033

[4]Larson, David, M.D., Editor-in-Chief: Mayo Clinic: William Marrow and Company, Inc., New York, New York, 1996, page 149 Title of book?

[5]IBID, Larson, page 149

[6]Anderson, Kenneth N.: Mosby's Medical, Nursing and Allied Health Dictionary, Mosby, Chicago: 1998, page 992.

[7]Klad, Michael J., M.D., M.P.H., Editor-in-Chief: John Hopkins, Harper-Collins Publishing, New York, New York, 1999, page 228 Title of book?

[8]Campbell, Robert J., M.D.: Psychiatric Dictionary. Oxford Press, New York, New York, 1996, page 425

[9]IBID, Campbell, page 425

[10]IBID, Campbell, page 425. He advocates Freudian psychology on sexuality

[11]Kaplan, Harold I., M.D. and Benjamin J. Sadock, M.D.: Synopsis of Psycharity, Williams and Wilkins Publishing, Baltimore, MD., 1991

[12]IBID, Kaplan and Sadock Page nos. for 11 and 12?

[13]Eysenck, H.J., W. Arnold and R. Meili, Editors:

Encyclopedia of Psychology, Seabury Press, New York, New York, 1979, page 629

[14]Craighead, W. Edward and Charles B. Nemeroft: The Corsini Encyclopedia of Psychology and Behavioral Science, John Wiley and Sons Publishing, New York, New York, 2001, apge 923

[15]www.religioustolerance.org article

[16]Life Bible Class Q&Z: www.bibleclass.com/mainpage/qa/qa6

[17]True Life Stories, "Living God's Way," Class 6: homepages.enterprise.net/bcfgoodnews/pages

[18]RBC Answers to Tough Questions: www2.gospelcom.net/rbc/questions/counsel/struggle

[19]What The Bible Says About Masturbation. Www.bible.com/answers/amasturb

[20]Dawson, McAllister. Christian Answers Network. Www.christiananswers.net/q-dmi/dmi-y011

[21]Pope Paul VI. Persona Human—Declaration on Certain Questions Concerning Sexual Ethics, issued by the Sacred Congregation for the Doctrine of the Faith, December 29, 1975.

Chapter Three

[1]Acts 25:16; 1 Cor. 9:3; 2 Tim. 3:15 where this concept is recorded in the Bible

[2]Dolphin, Lambert: Masturbation and the Bible: www.Idolphin.org/Mast/shtml

[3]IBID, Lambert

[4]IBID, Lambert

[5]www.family.org/docstudy/solid/a0014922.html

[6]IBID, Dobson

[7]Gallagher, Steve: At The Alter of Sexual Idolatry. Pure Life Ministries, Dry Ridge, KY., 2002

Chapter Four

[1]www.family.org/place/youand teens/a0020173.cfm

[2]www.religioustolerance.org/masturba2.htlm

[3]Ephesians 1:3-16

[4]IBID, Kaufman

[5]I Cor. 6:19-20; Phil. 4:8; Col. 3:17

[6]Paché, René: The Inspiration and Authority of Scripture. Translated by Helen Needham. Moody Press, Chicago, IL.: 1969, p. 102

[7]IBID: Encyclopedia of Psychology, p. 629

[8]www.family.org/docstury/sloid/a0014922/htlm

[9]IBID, Dolphin

[10]IBID: www.religioustolerance.com

[11]Goode, Bill. "Is All Truth God's Truth?" The Biblical Counselor's Newsletter

[12]IBID, Goode

[13]IBID, Goode

[14]I Cor. 11:1

[15]IBID: Psychiatric Dictionary

[16]The word "experts" represents the scientific, medical and psychological communities

[17]James 4:10-11

[18]The reader should not dismiss the associated sins because there is only one verse cited. One verse is still the verbal plenary voice of the Almighty. Due to limited space, other verses were not included.

[19]IBID, Gallagher, page 38

[20]Chafer, Lewis Sperry: Systematic Theology Volumne One, abridged edition. Victor Books, Wehaton, Il., 1988, page 140

[21]Isaiah 6:5

[22]Daniel 9:3-11

[23]Luke 5:8

[24]IBID, Gallagher, page 38.

Chapter Five

[1]Brown, Colin. Editor: International Dictionary of New Testament Theology, Volume 1 and 3. Zondervan Publishing, Grand Rapids, MI., 1975, pages 102, 104.

[2]IBID, Dolphin

[3]This phrase is used by Dr. John White in his book, <u>Eros Defiled</u>.

[4]Romans calls this conscience, creation, or the Living Word.[5]Remember Hebrews that speaks of the dullness of the saint living in sin.

[5]White, John. <u>Eros Defiled</u>. Intervarsity Press, Wheaton, Il. 1993, pages 124-125

Chapter Six
[1]Dt. 6:5; Mt. 22:27; Mk. 12:30; Lk. 10:27
[2]Personal Data Inventory Form
[3]Found in the <u>Christian Counselor's Manual</u>, Dr. Jay Adams, author
[4]IBID Adams <u>Christian Counselor's Manual</u>
[5]MacArthur, John Dr. and Dr. Wayne Mack, <u>Introduction to Bible Counseling</u>
[6]Pr. 23:7; Rom. 14:14; Js. 1:26
[7]Gen. 26:7. See also Nehemiah 6:9 and Philippians 1:17
[8]Eph. 5:18: Dan. 1:8; Col. ,3:2
[9]Ps. 26:2; Jer. 17:10
[10]2 Cor. 10:4-5. More about this will be said under Strength or the Disciplines for the person who masturbates.
[11]James 1:13-15
[12]These warning signs are basic to any temptation
[13]There are five biblical authorities: Church, Husbands, Parents, Employer, Government
[14]1 Cor. 10:31
[15]IBID, <u>Christian Counselor's</u> Manual
[16]1 Kgs. 11:2; Ps. 50:18; 1 Cor. 5:9, 11; 2 Thess. 3:14
[17]I am using small-sin groups as a descriptive phrase that describe popular self-help groups where the membership consists of people dealing with the same sin.
[18]Pr. 13:20
[19]Such transparency is harmful to new believers or carnal saints. See Romans 14 and 1 Corinthians, chapters 6-8 for passages on responsible living.
[20]2 Tim. 2:1-2

Chapter Seven

[1]When working with the husband, listen carefully for statements of the stability of his marriage in direct correlation to the frequency of sex. Husbands often equate a successful marriage with the frequency of sex with their mate.

[2]This may also be understood as storgé love. Listen to Dr. Ed Wheat's <u>Love Life Tapes</u>, cassette one.

**Study
Guide**

.

Chapter One

When you think or hear the word 'masturbation', what feelings or thoughts come to mind? Does the word make you uncomfortable? If so, why?

_____

_____

_____

_____

_____

_____

_____

Have you read any other literature on masturbation? If so, what did it say about masturbation? Did you agree with what was said? If so, why?

_____

_____

_____

_____

_____

_____

_____

The author writes, "It is not uncommon for masturbation to contribute to marital conflict." List several ways that masturbation could contribute to marital conflict.

_____

_____

_____
_____
_____
_____
_____

Many secular and Christian authors speak of 'courage' and 'compassion' in dealing with masturbation. Why does the author challenge this viewpoint?

_____
_____
_____
_____
_____
_____

Look up the word 'defraud" in a good collegiate dictionary. Write out all the possible definitions listed. Which definition comes close to showing masturbation's impact on the marriage relationship.

_____
_____
_____
_____
_____
_____

Look up the word 'defile" in a good collegiate dictionary. Write out all the possible definitions listed. Which definition comes close to showing masturbation's impact on the marriage relationship.

_____
_____

_____

_____

_____

_____

_____

Write out 1 Thessalonians 4:6. Read this verse in its context. What is Paul warning these Christians about?

_____

_____

_____

_____

_____

_____

Write out Hebrews 13:4. Read this verse in its context. Do you think masturbation defiles the marriage bed? How?

_____

_____

_____

_____

_____

_____

Record what you have learned from this chapter. Be specific.

_____

_____

_____

_____

_____

_____

Chapter 2

Summarize the medical community's viewpoint on masturbation.

_____
_____
_____
_____
_____
_____
_____

Summarize the psychological community's viewpoint on masturbation.

_____
_____
_____
_____
_____
_____

Summarize the religious community's viewpoint on masturbation.

_____
_____
_____
_____
_____
_____

List the six conservative Christian reasons that masturbation is a sin.

1._____
_____
_____

2._____
_____
_____

3._____
_____

4._____
_____
_____

5._____
_____
_____

6._____
_____
_____

Summarize the Roman Catholic position on masturbation.

_____
_____
_____
_____
_____

What are the four conclusions the author draws from these various viewpoints.

1._____
_____
_____

2._____

_____

_____

3._____

_____

_____

4._____

_____

_____

Explain the statement, "When you rule out God, you eliminate a viable, more understandable reason for the problem and liberating solutions."

_____

_____

_____

_____

_____

_____

Read Psalm 1:1-2. Answer the following questions.

What three things are we commanded to avoid?

_____

_____

_____

_____

_____

_____

What are we commanded to do?

_____

_____

_____

_____

_____

What does the word delight mean?

_____

_____

_____

_____

_____

_____

Read the following verses. Record what each verse says about **"WHAT NOT TO TRUST."**

Jer. 7:8 _____

_____

Psalm 118:9 _____

_____

Psalm 146:3 _____

_____

Pr. 3:5-6 _____

_____

What similarities do you see from these verses compared with what the medical, psychological, and portions of the religious community advocate?

_____

_____

_____

_____

_____

_____

Consult a Bible dictionary or concordance. Look up the word 'trust'. Summarize who we are to trust and why.

_____

_____

_____

_____

_____
_____
_____
_____

Read the following verses. What do they say about 'self-control'.

    Galatians 5:2-23_____
    2 Timothy 1:7_____
    1 Peter 1:13_____
    Titus 2:11-12_____

Read the following verses. What do they say about your 'body'?

    1 Corinthians 6:18-20_____
    Romans 14:7_____
    Romans 12:1_____
    Philippians 1:20_____

How valuable is God's Word? Read the following verses and record what they say.

    Psalm 119:9_____
    Psalm 119:11_____
    Psalm 119:24_____
    Psalm 119:29_____
    Psalm 119:37_____
    Psalm 119:45_____
    Psalm 119:99_____
    Psalm 119:128_____
    Psalm 119:130_____

Read Numbers 14. The 'majority rule' view is obvious. What was the majority view based upon? What consequences transpire because of the 'majority decision'?

_____

_____

_____

_____

_____

_____

    Record what you have learned from this chapter. Pay
careful attention to the study guide in the area of trust.

_____

_____

_____

_____

_____

_____

Chapter 3

List the nine arguments offered by the secular community condoning masturbation.

1._____
_____
_____

2._____
_____
_____

3._____
_____
_____

4._____
_____
_____

5._____
_____
_____

6._____
_____
_____

7._____
_____
_____

8._____
_____
_____

9._____
_____
_____

Explain the diagram and its significance.

_____
_____
_____
_____
_____
_____

The author writes, "What can be proposed for the majority who experience guilt and shame from masturbating?" Explain.

_____
_____
_____
_____
_____
_____

Complete this statement, "The problem with this line of reasoning..."

_____
_____
_____
_____
_____
_____

What Christian counselor aligns himself with the 'majority theory'? What significance do you think this endorsement has on the Christian home?

_____

_____

_____

_____

_____

_____

"The problem is the right of pleasure." What does this mean? What argument is this linked to?

_____

_____

_____

_____

_____

"Our society and its morés demand obedience to a code" . Explain this sentence.

_____

_____

_____

_____

_____

The author claims that surveys are not reliable. Why does he assert this?

_____

_____

_____

_____

_____

Steve Gallagher writes, "sexual sins are hidden." Explain further what he is referring to (page 24).

_____

_____

_____

_____

_____

_____

Write the definition for guilt_____

_____

_____

_____

_____

_____

_____

Write the definition for shame_____

_____

_____

_____

_____

_____

_____

How are they different?_____

_____

_____

_____

_____

_____

_____

Which one does the person who masturbates experience?

_____

_____

_____

_____

_____

_____

Do Christians have 'rights'? Why or why not? Support your answer from Scripture.

_____

_____

_____

_____

_____

_____

Read Psalm 139:7-12. What conclusion did the Psalmist reach about trying to hide from God? _____

_____

_____

_____

_____

_____

_____

What does Jeremiah 23:24 record about hiding from God?

_____

_____

_____

_____

_____

_____

Read Jonah, chapter 1. What ways did Jonah try to hide from God? Was he successful? Jonah 2 records the consequences of his attempts to hide. What happened to him, the boat, cargo, and sailors?

_____

_____

Chapter 4

List the ten statements used by the religious community to condone masturbation.

1._____

_____

2._____

_____

3._____

_____

4._____

_____

5._____

_____

6._____

_____

7._____

_____

8._____

_____

9._____

_____

10._____

_____

If the word 'masturbation' does not appear in the Bible, explain how can it be viewed as sinful?

_____

_____

_____

_____

_____

What is the problem with Dale Kaufman's scriptural boundaries? What important lesson should be observed when studying the Scriptures?

_____

_____

_____

_____

_____

Is all truth God's truth? Why or why not?

_____

_____

_____

_____

_____

From the life of Jesus, how should you imitate Jesus rather than a life of pleasure?

_____

_____

_____

_____

_____

List the biblical responses to someone who believes that masturbation is an acceptable replacement for fornication or adultery.

_____
_____
_____
_____
_____

Explain this diagram

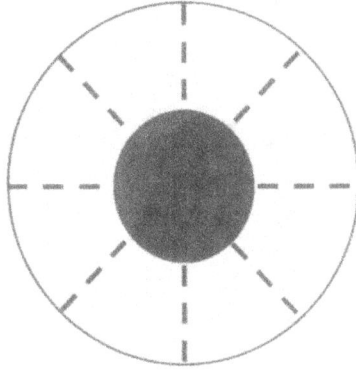

Why is this important when dealing with the sin of masturbation or any sin?

_____
_____
_____
_____

What do the following verses say about imitating Jesus as a Christian?

1 John 2:6_____

_____

_____

Ephesians 5:1-2_____

_____

_____

_____

_____

Demonstrate how a Christian focusing on God would find it impossible to masturbate.

_____

_____

_____

_____

Read Matthew 26:39. What was Jesus focus on? How would this help the person who masturbates?

_____

_____

_____

_____

Chapter 5

How does the author use the analogy 'closing arguments'?

_____

_____

_____

_____

List the various words and define them as used by others to find Scriptural support that masturbation is a sin.

1._____

_____

_____

2._____

_____

_____

3._____

_____

4._____

_____

5._____

_____

6._____

_____

7._____

_____

Which word best indicates that masturbation is sinful? Why?

_____
_____
_____
_____

What scriptural support is provided?

_____
_____
_____
_____

How does the author use 'biblical feelings' as a witness against masturbation?

_____
_____
_____
_____

How does the author use 'biblical focus' as a witness against masturbation?

_____
_____
_____
_____

Explain 'the concept of design' referred to by John White in his book Eros Defiled.

_____
_____
_____
_____

Other works by Dr. Thomas:

Worship: A Life in Tune with God
King David: God's Man with Feet of Clay
Restoring Truth to Counseling: Foundation for Change

You can access audio materials on a variety of counseling subjects by going to www.mtcarmelmin.org and click on "resources". There you will find individual cassette tapes, cassette albums, CD ROMs and printed study guides and booklets.

Dr. Thomas developed a correspondence course that when completed will start you on your way towards certification as a biblical counselor with the National Association of Nouthetic Counselors.

If you have questions for Dr. Rick, please e-mail him at mcmbclsor@juno.com.

To locate a biblical counselor in your area, contact the National Association of Nouthetic Counselors at info@nanc.org.